WE HAD FUN AND NOBODY DIED

WE HAD FUN AND NOBODY DIED

Adventures of a Milwaukee Music Promoter

Amy T. Waldman
with
Peter Jest

Foreword by David Luhrssen

WISCONSIN HISTORICAL SOCIETY PRESS

Published by the Wisconsin Historical Society Press
Publishers since 1855

The Wisconsin Historical Society helps people connect to the past by collecting, preserving, and sharing stories. Founded in 1846, the Society is one of the nation's finest historical institutions.
Join the Wisconsin Historical Society: wisconsinhistory.org/membership

Front cover image: Shank Hall photo: Bobby Tanzilo/OnMilwaukee

Unless otherwise noted, all images in the book come from the personal collection of Peter Jest.

Printed in Canada
Design and typesetting by Tom Heffron

28 27 26 25 24   1 2 3 4 5

Library of Congress Cataloging-in-Publication Data

Names: Waldman, Amy T., author. | Jest, Peter, author. | Luhrssen, David,
    writer of foreword.
Title: We had fun and nobody died : adventures of a Milwaukee music
    promoter / Amy T. Waldman, with Peter Jest ; foreword by David Luhrssen.
Description: [1st.] | Madison : Wisconsin Historical Society Press, 2024. |
    Includes bibliographical references and index.
Identifiers: LCCN 2023045683 (print) | LCCN 2023045684 (e-book) | ISBN
    9781976600302 (paperback) | ISBN 9781976600319 (e-book)
Subjects: LCSH: Jest, Peter. | Concert
    agents—Wisconsin—Milwaukee—Biography. | Rock
    concerts—Wisconsin—Milwaukee—History. |
    Concerts—Wisconsin—Milwaukee—History. | Shank Hall (Milwaukee,
    Wisconsin) | LCGFT: Biographies.
Classification: LCC ML429.J45 W35 2024 (print) | LCC ML429.J45 (e-book) |
    DDC 781.6609775/95 [B]—dc23/eng/20230929
LC record available at https://lccn.loc.gov/2023045683
LC e-book record available at https://lccn.loc.gov/2023045684

♾ The paper used in this publication meets the minimum requirements of the American National Standard for Information Sciences—Permanence of Paper for Printed Library Materials, ANSI Z39.48-1992.

To my mother and father, for believing in me even though they had no idea what this career entailed or how risky it would be.
—Peter Jest

To everyone who has ever experienced the sweet satisfaction of proving the naysayers wrong.
—Amy T. Waldman

Contents

Foreword

BY DAVID LUHRSSEN

I saw Peter Jest for the first time in 1973 at the private grade school we attended in Wauwatosa, Wisconsin. He was two years my junior, gawky and skinny, and looked like a kid other kids picked on.

Ten years later, he still looked like a kid—but not one to be picked on. One day in 1983, he cold-called to tell me about his venture into concert promotions. I was a gatekeeper in Milwaukee, musically speaking, in my dual role as critic for the daily *Milwaukee Journal* and editor at the monthly *Express* music paper. Peter was itching to get inside the gate. His recent debut as a concert promoter—a show by fusion band Spyro Gyra—was as uncool as could be from my perspective as a hip rock critic, and yet we kept talking.

I paid attention to him, in part, because of old school ties—almost as important in Milwaukee as in England. Equally, I was intrigued by his concept of booking bands into the University of Wisconsin–Milwaukee student union under the guise of a student organization. I had just become chairman of the student org that programmed UWM's Union Cinema and had learned something of the intricacies of promoting events to the general public from inside campus. UWM was a commuter school. Counting on students to fill seats was a loser's game. Peter was already president of the Alternative Concert Group, the name he'd chosen for his nascent student organization. I would soon become his vice president.

What struck me that day about Peter was that he wasn't going to be dissuaded by opposition—or bullied by anyone. If anything, he came armed and ready to muscle his way into the music business. Unlike the soulless corporations that gained control of much of the business nationwide, Peter loved music and knew a lot about the subject. But he was neither a musician nor a dreamy aesthete. He wanted to make his living in music—and needed to do it his way—because he couldn't imagine any other kind of life. We had that in common.

Peter pushed forward with his dream of becoming a professional concert promoter, despite the many obstacles he encountered. First were the unimaginative members of UWM's student government who were certain that music on campus should be limited to folk guitarists strumming in the corner of the student coffeehouse. Next came Milwaukee's musical old guard—promoters, disc jockeys, and critics rooted in the tail end of the '60s counterculture—who couldn't get past Peter's boyish eagerness. And finally, there were the postpunk hipsters who largely congregated on Milwaukee's East Side and turned their noses up at the kid whose musical tastes they deemed "mainstream" and very unhip.

One of my roles early on was as a bridge to the East Side crowd. I took Peter to a Purple Heart resale store and chose some cooler-looking clothes for him to wear. Peter went out on the town in costume at least once, but he soon returned to his fashion comfort zone—slovenly jeans and sweatshirts. More importantly, he consulted with me about the popularity of "alternative" musicians currently touring. Would high-decibel avant-noise guitarist Glenn Branca fill UWM's Merrill Hall? My advice was to go ahead; he listened. It was a memorable night with a good crowd.

Peter and I also worked together at the East Side location of a long since defunct record-store chain. It was a hipster hangout, and Peter got along well with a decidedly unconventional cast of coworkers. He was always listening to music, and while the esoterica of Dali's Car and Joy Division never dislodged Bob Dylan and the Rolling Stones from his pantheon, Peter's musical knowledge continued to grow. He was fired for no good reason during one of the store's periodic purges. I survived for another year until the axe finally fell on my head.

In 1984, we went to a theater to see a new film, *This Is Spinal Tap*, Rob Reiner's comedy about a fictional dysfunctional British rock band. In one scene, the band played a nonexistent Milwaukee club called Shank Hall. The other moviegoers sat mute throughout. We laughed continuously. Peter vowed that if he ever opened a club, he'd call it Shank Hall. And so it came to pass.

The Alternative Concert Group outgrew its UWM origins, and Peter became a go-to promoter for major acts across the musical spectrum, from Arlo Guthrie and Leonard Cohen to Patti Smith and King Crimson. Since 1989, at his East Side Milwaukee music club—yes, Shank Hall—Peter has catered to smaller touring acts, usually performers whose music he also enjoys. Peter accomplished his dream of breaking into the concert industry through diligence, persistence, and the determination to knock down—or the refusal to be knocked down by—any challenge that blocked his path. He was consistently irascible to anyone he deemed a foe and fiercely loyal to those he counted as friends. I'm pleased to be among the latter, and I found this book a truthful account of a remarkable career—one that might be impossible, given consolidation in the live-music industry, if he were that same kid starting out today.

1

The Contest Winner

Peter Jest's career as an independent music promoter almost ended before it began.

It was a Sunday night in the spring of 1984. Peter was nineteen, and it was his last semester as a full-time college student. For four semesters at the University of Wisconsin–Milwaukee, he'd paid tuition and bought books. Sometimes he'd even attended classes, written papers, and shown up to take exams. His grade-point average was a meager 1.4. That his grades were in the toilet didn't bother him the way it would most kids in his situation; his identity wasn't wrapped up in being a great student. It wasn't even wrapped up in being a student. But being a student was the only way to be president of a student group, and remaining president of his student group mattered a lot to Peter. Alternative Concert Group, which Peter had started at the university late in 1982, was dedicated to bringing national acts to campus. Running the group had given him the platform he needed to book and promote shows, and with every one of the nine he'd booked so far, Peter had learned something he could use to make the next one better. ACG was more than a reason to stay in school. It was the single most important thing in Peter's life. Now, using money he'd saved from his job at a gas station, along with his share of the proceeds from shows he and ACG had promoted with partners, Peter had made the jump. He had booked acoustic guitar legend Leo Kottke on his own.

It was Peter's name on the artist's contract, his name on the room rental agreement, his decisions to make when it came to setting the ticket price and organizing publicity. He'd ordered and paid for the sound tech, the stage crew, security, and bar service from the UWM student union. He'd

1

arrived five hours in advance of the 8:00 p.m. show. Now, he walked the rows of the Wisconsin Room, straightening a few chairs and noting the placement of the lights, making sure they were aimed properly. He greeted the sound engineer, then sent the stage crew off to perform a final inspection of the room. The platform stage held a single stool and two microphones. The sound engineer headed off to get a cold drink. He'd be back before Leo arrived and was set up for his 4:00 p.m. sound check.

At 4:15, there was no sign of Kottke. Peter was pacing the wide hallway, waiting for the man and his guitars to arrive on the elevator. According to everything he knew about Kottke, he was a professional and unfailingly prompt. Eyeing the closed elevator doors, Peter did his best to ignore what felt like a boa constrictor sliding down his throat to curl up in the pit of his stomach.

At 5:00 p.m., there was still no sign of Leo. No word, either. Peter walked back to the stage where he'd stashed his briefcase and checked the contract. Had he gotten the date wrong? He hadn't. Every time he walked between the room and the hallway, the walls seemed to close in another foot. The people around him knew better than to say anything or even come near him. He paced the room, thinking furiously while also trying

This ad for Peter's first Leo Kottke show was going to appear in the *Milwaukee Journal*, but ticket sales were good enough that Peter didn't need to run it.

not to think about what would come next. Faced with few alternatives, he continued moving forward as if there would actually be a show. Peter asked John Stropes, a guitarist friend of Leo's who'd shown up early to welcome him, if he'd stand in for the sound check. It might be a waste of time, but it made Peter feel like something was happening. At the very least, there would be decent acoustics, even if there was nothing to hear.

By 6:00 p.m., he allowed himself to do the math. With what he'd paid for the room and crew, plus refunding $8.50 × 400 in advance sales and factoring in what he'd have to turn away at the door, he stood to lose. . . . He didn't want to hit the total button on the calculator in his brain. At least he could say he'd tried. Now he'd probably have to find a real job, which, given the on-paper success of his college career, was going to be a challenge. He saw himself at forty, a single guy no one wanted to date, pumping gas on Milwaukee's far West Side, eating takeout in a one-room apartment, and falling asleep in front of old sitcom reruns.

And then a young woman in jeans was standing next to him beside the stage, surveying the end of his run as a music promoter. Row upon row of neatly arranged chairs, all empty. A perfectly ordered ruin.

"What?" Peter's question came out sounding like a growl, which he hadn't intended, especially because he realized he knew this woman. It was Janey Mohr, who ran the union's information desk, answering incoming calls.

She took a step back, let out a breath, and spoke. "They said you're Peter." She gestured back toward the door where the ticket taker was supposed to be stationed. The stage crew had settled there, as far from Peter as they could get without actually leaving the room.

He nodded. "Yes."

"You have a phone call at the desk."

He followed Janey out of the room and up the long flight of stairs to the information booth on the third floor. She handed him the phone. Standing in front of the counter, he closed one fist around the receiver. The other was clenched at his side. He took a breath and let it out.

"Hi, it's Peter," he said.

"Peter, it's Leo," Kottke said. "I missed the 94 turnoff in Madison, and I'm in Rockford. I'm turning around. I'll get to you as fast as I can. I'm really sorry."

Peter blinked, suddenly aware of how tightly his hand was wrapped around the phone. He took in what Leo was saying. Missed the turnoff? Missing the turnoff hadn't even made Peter's list of possible reasons for Kottke's no-show.

Peter let out a long breath. His grip on the phone relaxed, and his free hand fell open. "Um, oh," he said. "No. Thanks. It's okay. I mean, just get here safe, and we'll make it work."

At seven o'clock, when the doors opened, the line ran the length of the hallway. The room filled with the buzz of hundreds of small conversations as people walked to their seats, hands curled around their drinks. Their sense of anticipation was palpable—they had bought themselves a treat that was about to be delivered. Peter stood against the wall at the side of the room, his eyes moving between the scene in front of him and his wristwatch. Knowing that his artist was on the way was helping him breathe easier, but knowing Kottke wouldn't be there to be introduced on time left Peter unable to eat, despite the growing realization that he was hungry.

Shortly before Kottke was supposed to go on, Peter took the stage. "There's been a delay, but the show is still on. Thank you for coming, and thanks for your patience."

Around 8:30, Leo Kottke arrived at the union. Peter and John Stropes walked toward him as he emerged from the elevator, a guitar case in each hand. "I'm so sorry," he began, as they neared the stage entrance.

Peter raised his hands, gently brushing away the air in front of him. "It's okay," he said. "You're here now."

On stage, Kottke thanked the attendees for their patience as he tuned his guitars. For the next ninety minutes, he played, sang (in the voice he's described as sounding like goose farts on a muggy day), and told stories, including the one about the missed turn. Back home, after counting the door take, paying Leo, and walking him to his car, Peter sank into his bed, pulled up the covers, and fell immediately to sleep.

In 1971, Peter spent Christmas Eve in the emergency room. He could see the nurses' legs as they passed in the hallway but not much more; a curtain went all the way around his bed. He snuggled closer to his mother, looking at the pictures while she read the words of the book in her hands. Kathryn was reading E. B. White's *The Trumpet of the Swan* as she waited with her youngest son, passing the time until the doctor arrived.

> "Do you see what I see?" the swan whispered to her husband.
> "No. What?"
> "Over there. On that log. It's a boy! Now what are we going to do?"
> "How did a boy get here?" whispered the cob. "We are deep in the wilds of Canada. There are no human beings for miles around."

A nurse herself, Kathryn Jest had been monitoring seven-year-old Peter closely for the past week while he was home with a cough. Today, on Christmas Eve, she'd taken him to the emergency room as his asthma symptoms worsened.

Peter leaned back against his mother. He fell asleep to the sound of her voice as she read of the boy named Sam and Louis the swan, who taught himself to play jazz trumpet. When they got home later that night, she reread the parts Peter had missed. The next morning, Peter's presents were under the tree.

The Jest family would not have been out of place on a TV show. Think *Happy Days* meets *Leave It to Beaver* with a little *Father Knows Best* tossed in. Their tidy house on a tidy street in Milwaukee's Cooper Park neighborhood could have been the setting for any fifties-era sitcom.

The dad, Marvin, was a World War II vet who'd survived a German POW camp and gone to college on the GI Bill. He had an engineering degree that he'd put to work as a salesman for Auer Steel, a job that came with a company car. The mom, Kathryn, was a maternity nurse at Milwaukee Lutheran Hospital. She loved cross-stitching and collecting seashells. They were both pet lovers, but their son Tim's allergies and Peter's asthma meant no furry household pets. Re-homing the dog they'd had since before Peter was born was hard, but being able to visit occasionally and see him happy and cared for had taken some of the sting out of that painful but necessary decision. Like all good sitcom parents, their main focus was their children. Timothy was the eldest by nineteen months, then came Karen, Jonathan, and Peter, each spaced three years apart. They were fed and clothed, did their homework, and sat quietly in the pews at Our Redeemer Lutheran

Peter's parents chose this shot of their four kids (left to right, Jonathan, Timothy, baby Peter, and Karen) for the family Christmas card in 1964.

Church on Sundays. The Jests were a reassuring, ordinary family—the neighbors down the block, regularly referenced in conversation, who show up for a few on-camera moments every few episodes. All four Jest kids attended Our Redeemer Lutheran School through eighth grade and graduated from Milwaukee Lutheran High School. Timothy, Karen, and Jonathan got good grades and lettered in sports. In high school, Jonathan ran cross-country, Karen was on the pom-pom squad, and Tim played tennis. They went on to earn college degrees, each choosing a different role in the medical field. Tim became a doctor, Karen a nurse, and Jonathan a pharmacist. Tim and Karen married their high school sweethearts, Jonathan his college girlfriend.

Peter was different. With the exception of summertime Little League baseball, he didn't play sports. He never finished college. And he didn't get married for a long time.

Asthma meant taking it easy in gym class and Little League. His allergies meant weekly visits to the doctor's office for shots. Peter wished they could still have a dog, but other than that, life was pretty good. Riding his bike, playing with other kids in the neighborhood, and reading made him happy. He liked the Hardy Boys and the chapter books read by his mother when she tucked him in at night, or, if Kathryn was working a night shift at the hospital, read by his sister, Karen.

Peter was twelve when he inherited the paper route Tim had first passed to Jonathan. Now it was Peter's turn to get up at 4:00 a.m. to deliver the *Milwaukee Sentinel* to a hundred neighbors before school on weekdays and before breakfast on Saturdays. By this time, he was already walking around with a transistor radio in his back pocket. Listening to the radio was, at first, just another way to catch the Brewers, Bucks, or Green Bay Packers when he couldn't watch a game on TV. But at some point, while fiddling with the dial, his hand had slipped, and the hook of whatever pop song was playing had grabbed his attention. Soon, he was falling asleep to music on his bedside radio, listening in the car when he could get whoever was driving to turn to the station he wanted, and burning through nine-volt batteries the rest of the time.

In the car on the way to school or a doctor's appointment in the late 1970s, there was no way to be the tenth caller and win concert tickets, albums, or T-shirts. At 5:15 a.m., though, as Peter sat in the kitchen bagging newspapers, the red wall phone was in easy reach. One day, he dialed the station's number. Through the phone, he could hear Paul McCartney wonder what was wrong about filling the world with silly love songs. Then, the disc jockey cut in.

"Peter from Milwaukee is the tenth caller and wins a pair of tickets to see *The Omen!*" he said. "Hi, Peter!"

"Hi."

"What's your favorite radio station, Peter?"

"WOKY."

"Yes, it is! Stay on the line, Peter, and we'll let you know how to claim those tickets! We'll be giving more tickets away in the next hour, so keep listening, everybody! Now, here's 'Love Hangover' by Diana Ross!"

Once he'd cracked the code—a simple math equation—the prizes kept coming. If the disc jockey directed listeners to call 799-1234 and the fifth caller would be the winner, Peter simply added five to the last digit of the phone number, dialed 799-1239, and won. Since every station had multiple lines, everyone calling 799-1234 would be routed to the next line up. But by calling the winning line directly, Peter consistently had it tied up while everyone else was dialing in. To get around the rule limiting any given person to just one prize for a certain number of days, Peter used the names of his siblings and friends. His odds improved again when he

Before starting off on his paper route to deliver the *Milwaukee Sentinel* in 1976, Peter often called in to local radio station contests while bagging newspapers at the kitchen table.

convinced his father to replace the rotary dial phone in the kitchen with a push-button model. Peter programmed it to dial all the local radio stations, and their various phone lines, at the touch of a single button. He was the fifth caller, the fourteenth caller, the ninth caller.

In school, where he was an average but not particularly enthusiastic student, correct answers earned grades. On the radio, they generated prizes. Winning was better than buying, and prizes beat grades every time. Peter's favorite radio station became the one whose call letters he was reciting as he claimed the albums, movie passes, concert tickets, T-shirts, and signed photos.

Bob Seger became his first favorite artist after he won a complete catalog of Seger's albums. Peter was in eighth grade when Seger played Milwaukee. He and his friend Tim Scheuer bought tickets and went together. It was the first live concert for both of them. Peter had, by that time, enough life experience to recognize a transformational moment. Until that night, nothing he'd ever done had made him want to spend the rest of his life doing it. But everything about that night—the artist, the crowd, the energy, all of it—made him want to be where the music was. Not on stage, but involved in some way.

The morning after the show, Peter was back in the kitchen, ready to dial for prizes as he prepared to deliver the *Sentinel* before school. His taste evolved as his winnings increased, giving him the chance to hear more than just the radio hits of the artists whose albums he won and whose shows he was able to attend for free. He was too young to drive, but that wasn't an obstacle thanks to his parents, who dropped him off and picked him up from shows until he was able to drive himself.

It didn't take long for the word to get around at Milwaukee Lutheran that Jon Jest's little brother—the geeky-looking freshman with the fuzzy hair and the Sammy Hagar sweatshirt—had all the newest music and could get tickets to pretty much every concert in town. One of Jon's new cross-country teammates that year, Greg Koltermann, was also a freshman. When Greg first visited the Jests' house and descended into the basement, he found himself surrounded by albums—on shelves, stacked on tables, in piles on the floor. Music was everywhere. Greg and Peter spent hours there, listening to the radio and records, cementing a friendship that would lead them to attend countless live shows together over the next four years.

By 1978, the Jest family's basement was filling with prizes Peter had won from local radio stations.

≪ ≫

On a spring night in 1980, Peter sat in a booth at Petroff's, nursing a Miller High Life with his friend Mike and comparing notes about the Kansas show the night before.

He'd met Mike Wallander freshman year and the two had become fast, if visually improbable, friends. Peter was scrawny, five feet eight inches, and barely a hundred pounds. Mike was twice his size, taller, and two years older.

"Nice work on the second-row tickets, man."

"It pays to buy early."

"How'd you come out?"

Peter eyed the beer in his glass. At sixteen, he was too young to drink legally, but the bartenders at Petroff's Bowling Alley weren't picky about IDs. The gleeful shouts and loud groans of League Night mixing with the sound of falling pins echoed behind them.

"I did okay."

Mike nodded. He was used to Peter's secrecy around the profitability of his concert ticket business. But it had been a safe thing to ask, given the show, the seats, and the band. Also, once you knew Peter, it was easy to tell when he'd lost money. He didn't walk around yelling, but he exuded a definite "leave it" vibe when he was worried about recouping what he'd laid out in order to break even or make a profit. He financed the operation with money from his paper route and a weekend job pumping gas at Currie Park Auto on Highway 100 and Capitol Drive.

Peter would scour the papers for upcoming shows and make calls the moment tickets were available. As a member of the Stardate Concert Club, he could buy blocks of tickets before they went on sale to the general public. It also helped that he had a head start on seeing who was coming to town. All but three sections of the Sunday *Milwaukee Journal* were printed and ready on Saturday afternoon, which, thanks to Peter's friends with Sunday routes, is when he got the papers. He'd buy a block of seats, retain one for himself, and sell off the rest, using his dad's credit card to make the purchases and always paying him back before the monthly statement arrived. In addition to tracking his profit or loss from each show, he listed its promoter, venue, and overall attendance. For the Kansas show, he

Peter's membership in the Stardate Concert Club allowed him to buy premium seats to Stardate shows before they went on sale to the general public.

bought ten tickets at $105, sold nine for a total of $140, and netted $35. Earlier that month, he netted $2 for a sold-out Talking Heads show at the Oriental Theater on Milwaukee's East Side, buying six third-row tickets at $63 and taking in $65. Even if he could sell every ticket to a show, he always kept one for himself.

At Milwaukee Lutheran, it was common knowledge that Peter Jest was the go-to guy for the best seats to whatever touring band was coming through town. He was at every dance, not because he was popular with girls or had the best moves—he wasn't and he didn't—but because he had all the new music. He didn't play an instrument, but he was Milwaukee Lutheran's Music Guy. He was also Milwaukee Lutheran's Weekend Money Guy. Peter's very early version of a payday loan store was open for lending on Fridays, with payment due the following Monday.

"Hey."

Peter and Mike looked up.

"Do you know anyone who wants a hundred hot dog buns?" The bartender pointed to a box at the other end of the bar. "They got left out, and they're too stale to serve."

They looked at him. They looked at each other. Then their eyes lit up as grins sprouted. They knew exactly what to do with those buns.

Mike spoke first. "Koltermann!"

"We'll take 'em." Peter said. "Thank you."

They drained their glasses, grabbed their coats, hefted the box, and headed for Peter's car. It was a short drive from Fifty-Second and Burleigh to Greg's house.

The house was dark. Peter stopped the car, cutting the lights as Mike lumbered out of the passenger seat, box in hand. He opened the box and chucked the contents onto the Koltermanns' front lawn, moving as quickly as he could. Mike was panting heavily as he sank into the passenger seat, leaning to toss the empty box into the back seat.

Peter, taking a draw off his inhaler, wheezed with laughter.

They were still laughing when Peter dropped Mike off at his house.

The next morning at school chapel, Greg confronted Peter. "My dad woke me up yelling about my friends. He opened the curtains this morning, and there were, like, a hundred birds eating hot dog buns in the front yard, and he made me pick them up in the rain. He's sure it was either you or Ole Otto."

Peter played it straight. He shrugged. "Maybe you should ask Ole." Then he turned and walked off before Greg could catch him laughing.

Pranks and music were Peter's main avocations in high school, and he also managed the wrestling and track teams. He spent a significant chunk of his free time hanging out at local record stores—Radio Doctors in downtown Milwaukee and, closer to home, Peaches and Mainstream, both on the northwest side. He was one of a cadre of teenage music fans who spent more time talking to the clerks than spending money on records, mostly because he was winning a lot of what he wanted to hear. Robb Heilmann, the store director at Peaches, remembers coming in to work one morning after directing a staffer to swap out the Bruce Springsteen display for one featuring Michael Jackson's new release. Bruce was still front and center.

"What happened?" he asked the clerk.

"Peter wouldn't stop talking to me," the clerk said, "and by the time he left, I couldn't get it done."

"Next time," Robb said, "kick him out."

Between eighth grade and high school, as she'd done for his older siblings, Peter's mother had enrolled him in a typing course. She was thinking about the term papers and lab reports in his future. Instead, Peter used his typing skills to create itemized lists of his radio winnings, detailing dates, descriptions, and call letters of the radio stations whence they came.

From January 11 to August 15, 1979, for example, his winnings included *Steve Miller's Greatest Hits 1974–1978*; volume 2 of the *Beach Boys Greatest*

Hits, a T-shirt, and suntan lotion; *Move It On Over* by George Thorogood and the Destroyers; *The Very Best of Conway Twitty* and a frozen pie; a pair of tickets to *Fantastic Planet* (an animated science-fiction movie); eight Led Zeppelin albums; *Inner Secrets* by Santana; pizza, a wax job, two burgers, a six-pack of soda (cans), and two tickets to *Hair*; a double barbecue grill; two Heart tickets; two Kansas tickets; two tickets to Great America (an amusement park); two separate copies of *Where I Should Be* by Peter Frampton; *Whiteface* by Whiteface; two tickets to Summerfest; two tickets each to *A Hard Day's Night* and *Beatlemania*; two tickets to Rickie Lee Jones; a Skylab helmet; french fries; *Jazz* by Queen; two tickets to Steve Martin; two tickets to *The Muppet Movie* and a postcard; *Back to the Egg* by Wings; *The Texas Balladeer* by Freddy Fender; *State of Shock* by Ted Nugent, picture disc edition; *Rock On* by Raydio and a radio; two tickets to Joni Mitchell; and six tickets to the Allman Brothers (from different radio stations—four from one and two from another).

Between 1977 and 1982 when he stopped calling, Peter won more than 1,200 prize packages from local radio stations. He even helped his mother win a turkey one Thanksgiving. When she made it onto the air, the DJ said, "Hello," and she responded with "Gobble gobble!" The bird was hers.

In addition to the list detailing his ticket-scalping business and the other ones tracking how often he could call a radio station to win prizes and what name he should use, Peter had created a typewritten log of the shows he attended beginning in 1978. He listed the date, act, venue, and his seat. He also rated the show on a scale of 1 to 4 (in which 4 was as good as it gets and 1 was substandard). In May of 1982, with his high school graduation on the horizon, Peter cold-called a local promoter, Steve Mandelman. His concert-rating list had eighty entries; the scalping tally was sixty-five. Peter had originally thought he'd chase a career as a radio disc jockey. But now, he was thinking about a different idea. He'd been accepted to attend the University of Wisconsin–Milwaukee that fall. Mandelman was in the business. He lived close by, in Sherman Park.

"I have a book," he told Mandelman, "and I keep track of how all the concerts do. Would you like to see it?"

Mandelman invited the kid to come to his office, which turned out to be the third floor of his house. Ann Mandelman answered the door and called upstairs. Her husband appeared on the landing. Peter followed

PETER JEST PRODUCTIONS

Specializing in Concert Assistance

<u>Major Concerts I have attended</u>

<u>Rateings</u>

4-Excellent

3-Above Average

2-Average

1-Below Average

1978- 15 Concerts

1979- 6 Concerts

1980- 22 Concerts

1981 - 28 Concerts

1982- 30 Concerts

Date	Act	Venue	Rateing	
April 20,1978	Bob Seger,Sweet	Arena	3	M-RR
May 29,1978	Bob Marley,Imperials	PAC	3	21row
June 23,1978	America,Kate Taylor	Alpine	2	GA
June 24,1978	Shaun Cassidy	Alpine	1	GA
June 30,1978	Ted Nugent,Heart,Cheap Trick,Journey	Stadium	3	GA
July 2,1978	Alice Cooper,Eddie Money,Blondie	Alpine	3	GA
July 19,1978	Genesis	Summerfest Gr.	3	Ga
July 30,1978	Arlo Guthrie	PAC	3	12row
August 2,1978	Eagles,Steve Miller,Pablo Cruise	Stadium	4	GA
August 3,1978	Aerosmith,AC/DC	Alpine	1	GA
August 5,1978	Styx,Starcastle	Alpine	3	GA
September 1,78	Kenny Loggins	PAC	2	3balc
September 12,78	UFO,AC/DC,Bad Boy	Riverside	1	2balc
November 7,1978	Bread	Auditorium	2	19row
December 14,1978	Bob Seger,Southside Johnny	Arena	4	1strow

2863 North 90th Street   •   Milwaukee, Wisconsin 53222   •   **Phone: (414) 771-0561**

Starting in his teenage years, Peter kept three-ring binders with concert ratings, a log of his ticket resale business, and promotional copy for shows he'd attended. The concert ratings are typed, while the accounting of his ticket sales is neatly handwritten in blue ink on lined notebook paper.   •

Never a fan of having his picture taken, Peter fulfilled his high school graduation obligation by posing for this picture with his parents, Kathryn and Marvin Jest.

Mandelman up the stairs. He'd been nervous when he'd rung the bell, but now he was distracted by the round cloth disc on Mandelman's head. What did Jewish people call those hats again?

They reached the office. Mandelman sat at his desk and motioned for Peter to take a seat across from him. "So," he said, "your book."

Peter watched Mandelman examine the contents of the two three-ring binders he'd placed on the desk. Mandelman took his time, gently turning the loose-leaf pages. After what seemed like hours, he looked over at Peter.

"Why don't you hang around?" he said. "And how would you feel about working here? You could help me out a few hours a week."

The pay was nonexistent. Peter didn't care.

Mandelman was a couple of weeks out from a June 2 show. He was bringing John Mayall and the Bluesbreakers to the Performing Arts Center in downtown Milwaukee. The show was part of the band's Bluesbreakers Reunion Tour. Peter drove around town, distributing flyers. When Mandelman was busy, Peter answered phones.

The show was on a Wednesday. After school, he drove straight to the theater.

Backstage, he observed the preshow goings-on. When Mayall, Mick Taylor, John McVie, and Colin Allen went on, Peter was sitting in the audience using a ticket provided by his new boss. It was the first ticket in years that he hadn't bought as a part of his resale business or won in a contest. That Mandelman wasn't paying him didn't matter. Working for a promoter disqualified him from entering any more radio contests, but that didn't matter either.

He was still a week away from graduating high school, but Peter Jest had just turned pro.

2

That Won't Work Here

The bus ride to campus was long, but Peter didn't mind. He treated it as a rolling study hall, reading on the way there and back. He'd bought an orange 1978 Mustang II from his manager at the gas station, so driving to and from his classes at UWM was an option. But it wasn't a good option. Parking in campus lots was expensive. Street parking was cheap, but if you weren't plugging the meter religiously every two hours, it was a guaranteed parking ticket. Peter had better things to do with his time and money. His parents had laid out the terms before he started school: they'd pay for one semester, he'd pay for the next, then they'd switch off. What he saved on gas and parking would go a long way toward making sure he had enough saved before spring's tuition payment came due.

Between classes, he hung out at the student union, occasionally wandering the rows of tables run by various student organizations. Students were always there, standing or sitting behind their tables, ready to talk about nuclear disarmament, the literary magazine, endangered wildlife, or religious practice. It was a reliable source of pleasant and meaningless conversation.

He was taking three intro classes—Philosophy 101, Psychology 101, and Western History—and had upped his hours at the gas station to thirty a week. He was also working for Mandelman. He'd even gotten a paycheck. The Mandelman & Associates' show after the Bluesbreakers had been a Van Halen concert at Mecca Arena in downtown Milwaukee on August 17, 1982. Mandelman had offered Peter the runner job, a fifty-dollar gig that started at eight in the morning and ended after the show, whenever he was told he could leave.

A runner is basically the equivalent of a one-person firewall. Their main job is neutralizing Murphy's law—anything that can go wrong, will go wrong. If the roadies run out of duct tape while setting up the stage, the runner goes to the hardware store. If the tour manager arranged for laundry to be dropped at a cleaner's, the runner retrieves it when it's done. If the sound engineer needs a piece of equipment, the runner drives the engineer to the music store.

Among Peter's jobs that day was putting towels in the band's dressing rooms. After the show was over, he was tasked with retrieving and bagging them. (Mandelman's production manager would take them to be laundered the next day.) The doors had been hanging open earlier that day when Peter had walked in to place folded stacks on the counters. Now, he was retracing his earlier route, scooping used towels from the floor of the rooms vacated by Eddie and Alex Van Halen and Michael Anthony, scanning each room to make sure he hadn't missed any. David Lee Roth's room was last. Peter stepped inside, eyes tracking the floor for towels, when suddenly he

Peter's backstage pass from Van Halen's Hide Your Sheep Tour in support of the band's 1982 album *Diver Down*.

realized that instead he was looking at a pair of black leather pants and the guy wearing them was drying his hair with a towel. Peter scuttled out of the dressing room and back down the hall. The sound of Roth slamming the door behind him replayed in his head for most of the next day.

Mandelman's next show was Diana Ross, also at the arena. This time, he'd teamed up with Jam Productions, the biggest promoter in Chicago. Peter was the runner for that show, too.

Unlike at the Van Halen gig, a large curtain had been erected to run from the dressing room to the stage. Privacy was a serious matter for Ross. Peter had just completed an errand and was walking away from the stage when he noticed a man coming toward him. Peter stopped and stood, waiting until the man was close enough to say whatever it was he'd come over to say.

"You shouldn't be in the main arena when she's sound checking," he said. He was a well-built guy in a T-shirt that announced him as RTM Security. He delivered the information politely but with just the merest hint of a pause, as if waiting for an argument he wasn't sure he was going to get.

"I can go back to the room," Peter said, referring to the office used by the promoter's production manager the day of the show. "I'm just waiting for someone to give me something to do."

The fifty-dollar check he earned that day is long gone. But that exchange between Peter and Terry Cullen, who, as it turned out, owned RTM Security, was the beginning of a lifelong friendship.

The Van Halen and Diana Ross shows had been at the end of the summer. Now Peter was a student, juggling reading assignments and writing papers along with working concerts. Mandelman had teamed up with another promoter, Pat Casey of Sure Thing Ltd., to bring Van Halen to town. They were partnering again to bring Paul Anka to the Midwest in October.

The Anka shows were set for five dates in different cities throughout the month. Two of those cities were Milwaukee and St. Louis. Peter was already helping with flyers, phone calls, and logistics.

Everything was falling into place. And then, the Milwaukee Brewers and St. Louis Cardinals both won the pennants in their respective leagues. Suddenly, the World Series was all anyone could talk about in the Heartland.

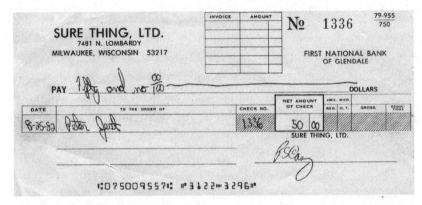

Peter's first check, issued eight days after he worked as a runner at the August 17, 1982, Van Halen show at the Mecca Arena.

Peter was the runner for the Milwaukee show on October 19. He'd spent the day at the Performing Arts Center, putting food and towels in the dressing room and being sent on various errands around town. It was a large-scale show. Two semi-trailers were parked at the loading dock; a bus had delivered the forty-piece band to sound check.

There was no curtain between the stage and the dressing room, so Peter watched as the band did its rehearsal and sound check without Anka. It was one of several unusual things he observed when he compared what he was seeing that day to what had occurred during the three previous shows he'd worked on. Peter focused on staying out of the way while remaining close enough to be readily available if Pat or Steve needed him, as he'd done with Mayall, Van Halen, and Ross. Today, though, he felt like anything short of invisibility was in the way. The production office was busier than he'd ever seen it. The phone would ring, Steve or Pat would answer, and the one with the phone to his ear would motion to the other to close the door. When a call ended, either the door would open to reveal them huddled together, making sure they couldn't be overheard, or the door would stay closed for an extended period of time.

Peter did what he always did when he knew he had nothing to contribute: he hung out in the hallway between the office and the stage, maintaining an intermittent watch on the office door. The hours passed and, eventually, Peter added peering out at what looked like a pretty sizeable crowd to his self-imposed to-do list. And then, the boss of the stagehands was standing in front of what turned out to be a live microphone. "I'm sorry, but due to unforeseen circumstances, tonight's show is canceled. Refunds will be available from wherever you bought your tickets."

Scattered applause and the occasional groan rose from the audience. Attendees gathered purses, jackets, and hats and left the theater, most of them in a hurry to get home and watch Game 4 of the World Series.

"Clear out what catering brought to the dressing rooms, and then you can go," Mandelman told Peter. "Just take it all home. I'll call you tomorrow."

When he got home with soda and sandwiches, his parents were in the family room, watching the game.

"Why are you home so early?" Marvin asked.

"You won't believe what happened," Peter answered. "But first, who's winning?"

What had happened was that two promoters and an occasionally paid intern found out how many Paul Anka fans in Milwaukee were also baseball enthusiasts. And they learned that, given a choice between a possibly once-in-a-lifetime event and a Paul Anka concert, once-in-a-lifetime won out.

Ticket sales had flatlined. Anka wasn't happy. Mandelman and Casey weren't happy. It's possible that their lawyers were also not happy. But they were definitely busy. Lawsuits were filed. Lawsuits were settled. When it was all over, Mandelman and Associates was out of business. So was Sure Thing, Ltd.

Not quite five months after he'd first knocked on Steve Mandelman's door, it looked like Peter's run as a promoter-in-training was over.

Shortly before the Anka debacle, Steve Mandelman had had a conversation with Warren Zevon's agent, a guy he knew well. The agent had asked Steve if he'd like to bring Warren to Milwaukee. "Ask around at UWM," Steve had told Peter. "I think it might be a good place for him to play."

Peter didn't have to think twice. National acts coming to school? That would be great. Students would love being able to see shows in a place on campus, somewhere that was close to where a lot of them lived. Plus, he was a Warren Zevon fan. It was an all-around win.

Peter made some inquiries, and then an appointment. The Union Activities Board (UAB) oversaw all student union activities and for coordinating events with student groups. It had an office down the hall from the UWM Ballroom.

Peter arrived at the appointment to find two upperclassmen, Darrell Kasper and Stephanie Busalacchi, at a table in the office. Kasper, who headed the UAB, sat with his arms crossed. Busalacchi, the concert chair, had a pad and pen. Peter took a breath and made his pitch. "I'm Peter Jest. It's my first semester here, but I know live music. I've worked for Mandelman and Associates and Sure Thing. We brought Van Halen and Diana Ross to Milwaukee," he said. "We have an offer to get Warren Zevon in Milwaukee, and I think that would work great here at UWM."

There was no hesitation. Kasper didn't even uncross his arms. "It won't work here," he said. "Nobody is going to come to UWM to see national acts."

Busalacchi looked as if she was about to say something when Kasper shot her a look. She stayed silent, glancing up quickly, then back down at her blank pad. It was pretty clear that the meeting was over.

Outside the door, Peter stood, bewildered, trying to process what had just happened. He left the union and walked around the block, becoming angrier with every step as he replayed the exchange. It had happened so fast. They hadn't even pretended to listen. They'd just dismissed him out of hand, as if he didn't know what he was talking about, as if he didn't matter, as if he were one of those clueless students standing in the union asking questions about joining the Baseball Club.

Two weeks later, he was still fuming over what had happened at the union. And now, worse, his link to the concert world was gone.

And then, it hit him. A student group. He could start a student group to put on concerts. One of the tables in the union that first week of school had been offering info about how to start student groups. He vaguely remembered being handed a packet, which he'd taken to be polite.

That night at home, he riffled through the stack of papers that had been growing taller every time he'd emptied his backpack. It was there. He needed a group name, purpose, and the signatures of four people who were willing to serve as officers.

In short order, three Milwaukee Lutheran classmates also attending UWM had signed on as vice president, secretary, and treasurer of Peter's group. On November 7, he walked the completed paperwork to the Dean of Students Office and waited.

Then, in early December, a letter arrived from the assistant dean. Alternative Concert Group was an approved UWM student organization, with the rights and responsibilities thereof.

Peter let Steve Mandelman and Pat Casey know, but separately. Their relationship had been a casualty of the Anka debacle. Pat helped Peter connect with two bands, Spyro Gyra and the Outlaws, who could potentially come to UWM the following spring. The bands were already playing dates in Green Bay, so getting them to Milwaukee was a realistic possibility.

Spyro Gyra wanted $7,500. The UWM Ballroom, the largest venue to which Peter had access, seated 750. That was ten dollars a ticket, without even accounting for the other expenses he'd incur. It was unaffordable. Unless, Pat pointed out, the band was willing to play two shows for that amount.

Peter asked.

They were.

The shows were scheduled for seven and nine o'clock on March 7, a Monday night. Administrators and members of the student government were sure it would be a train wreck.

It was early December, and Peter's first semester was nearly behind him. He'd started college as a promoter's assistant. Now, he had his own shows to plan. He was still working his gas station job, and that money would help to finance his new adventure. Finals week came and went. His first semester GPA was 1.92—a C in history, a C– in philosophy, and a D in psychology.

Over the semester break, Peter got to work. He'd booked the Ballroom. But between the end of December and the day of the show, he had to arrange for stage setup, room setup and cleanup, lighting, catering, security, tickets, advertising, a sales permit, and, as outlined in the band's contract, a piano tuner the day of the show. Most important, he needed to make sure he sold enough tickets to pay for it all.

It was late 1982. There were no cell phones. No internet. No laptop computers. No e-tickets. Promoters ordered tickets from specialized companies. Steve and Pat used Ticketcraft in Bellmore, New York, so Peter called Ticketcraft and ordered four sets, in separate colors with slightly different wording. Student tickets, priced at $7.50, would be available only

THE UNIVERSITY OF WISCONSIN—MILWAUKEE/P.O. Box 413, Milwaukee, Wisconsin 53201

DIVISION OF STUDENT SERVICES AND SPECIAL PROGRAMS
OFFICE OF THE DEAN OF STUDENTS

November 30, 1982

Peter Jest, President
Alternative Concert Group
2863 N. 90th St.
Milwaukee, WI   53222

Dear Peter Jest:

This is to inform you that the _____

 Alternative Concert Group

was chartered by the Student Association on__ November 21, 1982 __

and the Office of the Dean of Students on __ November 22, 1982 __

Being a fully chartered UWM student organization, you are entitled to all
privileges as outlined in the Student Organization Handbook. To maintain
your charter it is necessary that you complete registration forms each
semester and report any changes in your list of officers or Constitution
to the Office of the Dean of Students when they occur. Every student
organization must have a Union mailbox in order to receive official
notices, etc. Please come to Mellencamp Hall, Room 118 to pick up your
assigned mailbox number and combination.

If I can be of any help to your organization and its activities, I am
eager to do so. Best wishes for future success.

Sincerely,

Bob Trotalli
Assistant Dean

RJT:jbh

cc: Reservations
    Advisor

More than any of the classes he took in college, Peter's position as president of
Alternative Concert Group and the accompanying "privileges as outlined in the Student
Organization Handbook" gave him an education in how to become a successful music
promoter.

Miller Brewing & Alternative Concert Group
Present

SPYRO GYRA

In Univ. of Wis.-Milwaukee Union Ballroom

MONDAY MARCH 7, 7:30 P.M. and 9:30 P.M.

Tickets on sale at UWM BOOKSTORE, Radio
Doctors, Main Stream and Ludwig Von Ear

7.50 students   9.50 public

In March 1983, Peter was still a member of the Stardate Concert Club and still keeping a log of shows he'd attended; this ad for Spyro Gyra was the first one he added for a show he'd booked himself.

at the UWM Bookstore. Everyone else would pay $9.50, and those tickets would be made available at locations throughout Milwaukee.

When the spring semester started, Peter began lugging a briefcase to campus along with his backpack. Inside was everything he needed to keep preparations straight for the four acts he'd booked that semester. In addition to Spyro Gyra and the Outlaws, he was promoting Roger McGuinn, the former front man of the Byrds, who'd been touring regularly as a solo act since the band's breakup a decade earlier. He'd also booked Einstein's Riceboys, a local band.

Some people noticed the skinny kid with the huge briefcase as he walked in and out of lecture halls and dorms, but mostly Peter was ignored as he scoured campus for bulletin boards. Stopping when he found one, he'd kneel and reach into the briefcase, pulling out a poster and flat of thumbtacks. He'd tack the poster to the board, slide the tacks back into the briefcase, and move on. He drove around town, hanging posters in the same places he'd gone when he worked for Steve, making sure to pay special attention to the businesses around campus.

ACG didn't have a campus office, so the Jest family basement became ACG's base of operations. There, Peter stuffed envelopes to mail to media outlets and followed these up with phone calls. He bought ads in both daily papers, the morning *Milwaukee Sentinel* and the afternoon *Milwaukee Journal*; the alternative weekly, the *Crazy Shepherd*; and the *UWM Post*, produced by another student group.

At the beginning of February, Peter began distributing tickets. He hand-delivered fifty of each type to the UWM Bookstore and dropped the general-admission tickets at local record stores. He left 175 for each show at Radio Doctors, 125 for each at Mainstream, and 50 for each at Ludwig Van Ear and Peaches. He called each location on Mondays, Wednesdays, and Fridays to check on sales. If an outlet's supply was fewer than ten, he'd drop off another fifty.

Between replenishing tickets at record stores and organizing logistics for shows, Peter was still putting in thirty hours a week at his gas station job while also attending classes. History 285, about the Pacific theater of World War II, was the most interesting because his father had been a POW in Germany. The class was a chance for Peter to learn more about what had occurred during that time and possibly answer some questions he hadn't known to ask. His other two courses, Public Speaking and American Politics: The National Scene, were less compelling. Sitting through those lectures felt like listening to elevator music—he was dimly aware of the background noise as his mind drifted, contemplating ways to sell more tickets to his planned shows and coasting along on a sea of ideas about other acts he might bring to campus.

February rolled into March. Then, it was show day. ACG's officers—Jody Bartell, Tim Scheuer, Paul Beilke, and Jon Schrank—served as the stage crew, helping with load-in and setup.

The union staff had set up the largest stage available, making sure to leave room for the lights. The room was set up for maximum capacity, 750 seats, audience style. Union personnel were working catering for Spyro Gyra, as well as security and the bar for attendees. The union didn't have a sound tech, so Peter had hired a professional. He knew when the band would arrive and what time they wanted to do sound check.

Ticket sales had been brisk, so Peter was pretty sure things would be all right. Still, he was anxious. A lot of people seemed interested in seeing him fail. He hoped not to give them the satisfaction. It was a hope he realized.

Both shows sold out, breaking a record for the biggest draw for a show at the UWM Union. Pat Casey's brother-in-law, Alan Dulberger, was in the audience. He had been one of Milwaukee's pioneering promoters in the early 1970s—co-owner of Daydream Productions with his partner, Randy McElrath. After they split, they promoted shows individually—Alan as Landmark Productions and Randy as Stardate Productions. They'd brought Pink Floyd and a host of other bands to Milwaukee in the 1970s before splitting.

After the show, Alan waited around until Peter was available. "You've got a great thing going here," he said. For Peter, having the guy who'd been involved in bringing Pink Floyd to Milwaukee (twice!) attend his show was a big deal, but for that guy to offer what was basically a benediction added extra shine to an already big moment.

Peter's file from that night includes a two-column list on a single sheet of loose-leaf paper. Written in blue pen under Spyro Gyra is an itemized list of expenses and receipts. The cost of achieving the impossible, it turned out, was $11.80, the amount Peter lost on the show.

ACG's second show occurred the following Saturday in the Ballroom. It was much more of a low-key affair. Einstein's Riceboys was a local

Peter's handwritten accounting on loose-leaf paper shows that he lost $11.80 bringing Spyro Gyra to the UWM Union in 1983.

band, performing for $500, a fraction of what Spyro Gyra had cost. Peter partnered with the band to get the word out and posted flyers around campus. Attendees paid at the door. There was no need for the group's officers to be there, although they were always welcome. Total costs for the show were $1,137.93; net receipts were $655.50. Peter wasn't making money, but what he was learning was worth the $482.43 loss.

Peter had two more shows that semester. Roger McGuinn went well, but the Outlaws show was a disaster. Peter had followed the Spyro Gyra formula, peppering campus and the community with flyers, buying ads, reaching out to the media. But tickets weren't selling. When show day rolled around, he didn't have enough to pay the band.

He called the promoter in Green Bay to ask if he'd advance the money and let Peter pay him back. The answer was no, served up with a chaser. "You've got to come up with the money to pay them or they won't go on," the promoter told him.

Peter had seen that outcome once and knew the last thing he wanted was to see it again, especially with himself in a starring role. Ticket sales weren't something he could control, but that didn't matter. He'd signed the contract. He was responsible.

He left campus, went to the bank, and drained his account of nearly all the money he'd saved from his paper route and the gas station. If he didn't pay the band, he knew it would ruin his reputation and he'd never get another show. He had already learned—if a promoter doesn't keep his word, he's not going to stay in business. And he figured this would be especially true for an eighteen-year-old with no longevity to his name.

There was something else, too—something important enough that using his life's savings to avoid it would be money well spent. He wouldn't have to hear anyone say, "I told you it would never work."

The Outlaws got paid. The show went on.

Emptied bank accounts aside, Peter was grateful to have been able to bring Spyro Gyra and the Outlaws to UWM that spring. He had learned a lot. But the fact that he'd learned anything that semester might have surprised his professors. His GPA that May was 1.33.

That summer, Peter spent time working on the package he'd be submitting to UWM's Student Association to receive approval and funding for ACG in the 1983–84 school year.

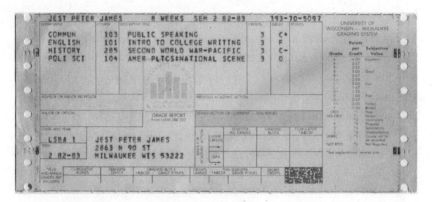

Academic excellence was not Peter's priority at UW–Milwaukee.

The Senate Finance Committee, part of the Student Association, allocated segregated fees paid by all students as part of their tuition to student groups, which received amounts ranging from less than twenty dollars for some small groups up to many thousands of dollars for groups like the Student Legal Clinic. Peter's pitch was written on Alternative Concert Group letterhead.

> As an organization, ACG has earned the respect—as attested to in letters of recommendation—[of] full-time music reporters at the *Journal*, *Sentinel* and *Express* as well as agents and promoters, for the professionalism of its operation.
>
> Beside servicing the recreational needs of UWM students, ACG is providing training for large numbers of students interested in pursuing such music-related careers as stage hands and public relations specialists.
>
> We believe that $7,500 in segregated fees recommended by the SFC is the minimum needed to continue the program envisioned by ACG for UWM students. Your support is necessary if national entertainment is to remain a reality on our campus.

Peter enclosed letters of recommendation from Mark Shurilla, editor and publisher of the *Express* music magazine; Dave Luhrssen, freelance journalist and Peter's UWM classmate; and the pop music reporters from both daily newspapers. He also submitted letters from Steve Mandelman and Pat Casey.

ACG was awarded the $7,500. Now, Peter had a solid seed budget and the resources of the university. He reregistered for Public Speaking and signed up for two intro courses, Sociology and College Writing. But classes, again, took a distant back seat to planning his shows. Peter was too busy doing what his classmates were reading and writing papers about. And he was getting good at it. If he could secure a venue for an act he wanted to book, then he'd send an offer to the band including a dollar amount, date, and venue. If the band's agent responded, and the answer wasn't no, then negotiations ensued.

Bringing Spyro Gyra to campus had been a way to test a hypothesis: People would come to UWM to see live music performed by nationally known artists. He was a kid trying to see if he could make something happen and prove his naysayers wrong.

The naysayers, though, weren't pleased at being shown up by an eighteen-year-old who looked like he regularly slept in his clothes.

When Peter reserved the Ballroom for three of the four shows he wanted to bring to campus in the fall of 1983 (the fourth, Glenn Branca, would be in a different building), someone in Union Programming passed the information on to the UAB concert chair. It was Stephanie Busalacchi, the person who'd sat silently when Darrell Kasper had dismissed Peter out of hand a year earlier.

His offer to Vital Information (a side project of Journey drummer Steve Smith) went as expected. He'd also made offers to the Romantics and the Violent Femmes. When Peter reached out to their respective agents to follow up on those offers, they responded that they'd since received offers to play the Ballroom on those dates from the UAB—and for more than Peter was offering.

To add insult to injury, the UAB hadn't made the offer directly. The concert chair had gone through a middle agent, adding additional costs to an already large offer.

Peter was outraged on multiple fronts. The targeted attack on his group (which, to be honest, was largely a solo act) was bad enough. But even worse was the fact that the UAB was using student money to wage this bidding war, and for no reason he could see beyond trying to put him in his place.

The war remained a cold one, with the battlefront confined to negotiations between the bands and the groups vying for the dates. There were no confrontations.

Ultimately, Peter got both shows. They came at a higher cost than he'd initially offered, but lower than the concert chair's offers. For the Romantics, he partnered with Union Programming. That group was run not by students but by paid professionals, who booked films, lectures, and other events in the main concourse. Scott Gore, who ran the office, was intrigued by what Peter was trying to do. They split costs and duties, and the show sold out.

For the Femmes, Peter turned to local disc jockey Dan Hansen, a.k.a. "Downstairs Dan," with whom he'd copromoted the Roger McGuinn show earlier in the year. Hansen also did some side work as a promoter. Peter asked for help. Hansen knew the band, which tipped the balance in Peter's favor. The show was a hit, but the *Milwaukee Journal*, then the state's biggest paper, got the date wrong, resulting in a crowd that was smaller than it would have been otherwise.

In December of 1983, Peter wrote a letter to the president of the Student Association detailing the events leading up to the Femmes show. It is a vivid illustration of how willing he was to push back on anything that got in his way.

> Many people had talked about bringing the Femmes in. The Alternative Concert Group made a bid on them for a Friday night for $1,800. They were going to accept. Upon telling [a member of the programming staff] in confidence, she then proceeded to tell [the UAB. The concert chair] then made her bid for a Thursday night for over $2,000. Upon hearing this, I talked with members of the Student Association to let them know of the waste of students' money. . . . I dropped out of competition for the Violent Femmes.
>
> Following this, the UAB needed funding for the concert. So, thinking again of the students, we decided to put some of our money into the show along with Union Programming. UAB was handling all the negotiations.
>
> The negotiations were messed up. The agent did not know what was going on and, coming to the breaking point, canceled the show. All three programming departments agreed, since the principle of giving someone $200 after supposed verbal agreement is wrong. It was the principle, not the money. But the agent did have valuable

questions. The first offer was around $2,200, then $1,700 plus 50 percent gate, then $1,700. I would have canceled too if I was the agent.

The next day, I received an offer for the Violent Femmes. The price had gone up because of UAB's original bid. I was hesitant to do the show and (told them) I would call them back. I went ahead with the show.

The last paragraph of the draft is crossed out: "To condense: The UAB messed up, we took over and succeeded. We know they are jealous and after us. Well, the ACG refuses to have a battle of wits with unarmed people."

In years to come, Peter wouldn't have to compete with anyone inside an organization he was working with to put on a show. But in all aspects of his life, the best way to encourage Peter to do something was to try to stop him from doing it.

3

Pissing Next to Batman

The truth was simple. He had no business staying in college. After three semesters, Peter had the track record—and the grades—to prove it. Academically speaking, he was a failure. Socially, things were pretty much the same as they'd been in high school. He watched sports and sitcoms with high school buddies Mike and Greg, got turned down almost every time he plucked up the nerve to ask a girl out, and hung out with a couple of friends he'd made as a result of his shows. One, Dave Luhrssen, had been a classmate of Peter's brother Jon at Our Redeemer and Milwaukee Lutheran. A history major and film buff who loved music as much as Peter did, Dave had agreed to sign on as Alternative Concert Group's vice president for the fall 1983 semester.

Leaving school, though, wasn't an option. The rules were clear about that. Student organizations were, by definition, "comprised and controlled by students enrolled at the University of Wisconsin–Milwaukee." Once a group was formed and approved, the university assumed that it would function as a unit, with its officers running things and its members providing input and support.

Peter's former classmates from Milwaukee Lutheran had readily signed on to help him form the group. Having benefited from his radio winnings and his ability to score seats at shows, they were at the ready to sign whatever was necessary to keep the group going, help with show setup, and do anything else he needed. But Peter didn't need much. Other students who expressed interest in joining were welcomed, but few did. Peter was too busy putting together shows to host a table at the union, and it never occurred to him to recruit members. He booked the shows, he and Dave handled publicity, and Dave wrote press releases and ad copy. Rather than rely entirely on the allocation ACG received from the Senate Finance Committee, Peter used his own money to bring bigger acts to campus, reserving the segregated fee funding for more esoteric acts, among them singer-songwriter-producer T-Bone Burnett and jazz composer Sun Ra and his Arkestra. Alternative Concert Group wasn't a group by any conventional definition of the term.

Early on, Peter had figured out that he needed a way to break into the concert business, and he'd reached out to Steve Mandelman. It had gotten him to where he was now. But his lackluster performance in the classroom didn't attract any attention from his professors, and the idea of sitting down with an academic adviser to talk about what he was doing never occurred to him. Had it, it's possible that Peter could have continued what he was doing with an independently designed cross-disciplinary major. Peter's work putting together shows combined elements of business, economics, sociology, psychology, and communications. His work with Dave showed his ability to collaborate and delegate tasks. The results were tangible. Peter was doing poorly in the classroom but he was excelling at getting an education.

In February of 1984, he brought T-Bone Burnett to the Wisconsin Room. In April, he put on three shows: guitarists Leo Kottke and Daryl Stuermer, and blues singer and guitarist John Hammond. In May, the Violent Femmes played the Ballroom again, this time with the correct

The Violent Femmes performing in the UWM Ballroom on May 2, 1984. Left: Gordon Gano (foreground) and Victor DeLorenzo (background). Right: Brian Ritchie.
PHOTOS BY SCOTT RUUD

ACG's second Violent Femmes show opened with Milwaukee-based punk rock band Couch Flambeau, who also opened Peter's show for the Replacements later that month.
COURTESY OF MILWAUKEEROCKPOSTERS.COM/RON FAIOLA

date printed in the *Milwaukee Journal*. That month, Peter also brought Minneapolis-based rockers the Replacements and bluesman Robert Cray to campus. Finally, in June, he closed out the semester with punk rock, American finger-style guitar music, and good old rock 'n' roll with the Jim Carroll Band, John Fahey, and the Steve Morse Band, respectively.

Between the Steve Morse show on June 22 and Peter's next date came another pivotal career moment. Steve Mandelman had recommended Peter to his friend Bob Babisch, the entertainment director at Summerfest.

Since 1970, the annual music festival on an eighty-acre former missile site at the eastern edge of downtown Milwaukee on Lake Michigan has drawn thousands of Midwestern music lovers of all ages and from all walks of life. Within a tiny radius of anywhere on the grounds, attendees are almost guaranteed to find a live performer or band on one of the festival's ten stages playing something they want to hear.

Babisch hired Peter to manage the Matilda Bay Stage. For the eleven days of the festival, Peter arrived at 10:00 a.m. and left after midnight, doing the same thing he did at his UWM shows but with one big difference: he was only doing the production component. Five times a day, a band loaded in, went on, got off, loaded out, got paid. The first band went on at noon; the headliner started at 8:00 or 9:00 p.m., depending on the day. It was Peter's job to make sure everything ran smoothly and according to schedule, and he did it well.

Summerfest ended on July 8. Just three days later, July 11, turned out to be a banner day in Peter's life. That April, he and Dave Luhrssen had gone to see *This Is Spinal Tap* at the Mill Road Cinema. While most moviegoers in the crowded theater sat silently in confusion, Dave and Peter laughed their way through the mockumentary about a trio of aging rockers on a reunion tour. One scene featured Spinal Tap's stop at a fictional club in Milwaukee called Shank Hall. At that venue, they performed a song called "Stonehenge" in front of a laughably small eighteen-inch model of the famous standing stones.

Peter leaned over to Dave. "If I ever open a nightclub," he said, "I have to call it Shank Hall. All the musicians will love it."

A month later, when Peter learned Spinal Tap was doing a tour that included Boston, New York, Chicago, and Los Angeles, he contacted the band's publicist. Noting Milwaukee's proximity to Chicago, as well as

Michael McKean's tie to the city as an actor in the Milwaukee-based *Happy Days* spin-off *Laverne & Shirley*, Peter made an offer that could only work in Milwaukee.

"If they come," he said, "I'll rename the UWM Ballroom Shank Hall."

It was three thousand dollars well spent. With the date set, Peter called the mayor's office and got the city to issue a proclamation declaring July 11 Spinal Tap Day. He also commissioned an eighteen-inch replica of the Stonehenge stones to hang in front of the stage. The band stayed in character onstage and off. As Spinal Tap's guitarist Nigel Tufnel, Christopher Guest grabbed Peter by the collar in a rage when the sound system he'd rented for the band didn't work properly. At the end of the night, when he paid Michael McKean, playing his character of lead singer and guitarist David St. Hubbins, Peter told him how much he'd loved him as Lenny Koslowski in *Laverne & Shirley*. "That's a different person," McKean said.

Two other things made the Spinal Tap show a standout. The first was Bruce Springsteen. The same night as the Spinal Tap show, Springsteen was in town. He'd arrived a day early before a stop on his *Born in the USA* tour at Alpine Valley, the outdoor amphitheater just southwest of Milwaukee

A peak moment in Peter's career was securing a previously unscheduled Milwaukee date on the 1984 Spinal Tap tour. He ordered up a tiny replica of the Stonehenge stones and turned the UWM Ballroom into the film's fictional Shank Hall for a night.

The members of Spinal Tap at the 1984 show in Milwaukee included (back row, from left) Harry Shearer, David Kaff, Michael McKean, and Christopher Guest, as well as Ric Parnell (center front). Peter is standing in the back row at far right with *UWM Post* photographer Annie Belke in front of him. PHOTO OF ORIGINAL BY EROL REYAL

in East Troy. Two hours before Spinal Tap was scheduled to start, Peter got a call from Dallas Cole, a WKTI disc jockey he knew. Cole was also the station's program director.

"Springsteen's people just called to get directions to your show," he said. Peter didn't even try to play it cool. He thanked Cole and practically danced back to where the band was sitting.

"Bruce Springsteen might be coming," he told them. "Could we set up a microphone and have him play with you if he wants to?"

Back and forth they went, in character, discussing at length whether or not Springsteen would be welcome. "I guess if he shows up," Tufnel finally said, "we can let Bruce play with us."

Springsteen, for the record, didn't show. But Peter did get sued.

A student attendee was angry that the band went on too late. After two opening acts, the Spinal Tap crew had taken a bit of extra time to get their makeup right and went on later than planned. The student filed a complaint with the university. When they met in Student Court, the plaintiff was awarded $10. It was the perfect coda to Peter's Spinal Tap experience.

That wasn't ACG's only movie-related show that year. While flipping channels at home earlier that spring, Peter had come across a broadcast of the 1966 movie *Batman*. In it, Batman and Robin thwart the plans of Catwoman, the Joker, the Riddler, and the Penguin to hold the world ransom using a secret invention that can instantly dehydrate people. Peter had gotten Spinal Tap. Why not Adam West? Batman 101. Show the movie, get Batman to give a lecture.

With Summerfest behind him, Peter tracked down West's agent, a man named Lew Sherrell, who represented a slew of 1960s and 1970s TV and movie stars. He dialed the number.

"I'm Peter Jest with Alternative Concert Group," he told Lew, strategically omitting the parts about being nineteen and calling from his parents' basement. Sherrell said he'd run the idea by West and get back to Peter. A week later, he had an answer. Adam West was interested.

It was a busy summer. Peter was working full-time at the gas station. He was also arranging a more robust schedule of shows at UWM. In August, Peter turned twenty. Kathryn made his favorite dinner—meat loaf, and, as always, pumpkin pie for dessert, which Peter preferred to birthday cake.

The semester started with Peter auditing three one-credit classes: Weather Maps, Snowstorms, and Milwaukee's Weather. As an enrolled student, he remained eligible to run his student group. Between September 10 (the David Murray Octet) and December 5 (Lite Comedy, a Miller Lite comedy show), ACG brought twenty shows to campus.

One, a sold-out show on September 27, was particularly rewarding. A little less than two years earlier, in the Union Activities Board office, Darrell Kasper and Stephanie Busalacchi had dismissed the idea of Warren Zevon playing at UWM, assuring Peter that no one would show up. The ensuing two years had brought some real successes (and a few setbacks) for Peter. But as he watched Warren Zevon play to a full house in the Wisconsin Room, his face lit up with a smile that wouldn't quit. Every note of that show was the sweetest-sounding middle-finger salute he'd ever heard.

Several days later on October 2, Peter got to spend one day as a runner for Sammy Hagar. This was a couple of years before Hagar joined Van Halen. It was a big deal for a kid whose high school nickname had been "Sammy" on account of the Hagar sweatshirt he'd won in a radio contest and wore to school that often.

It took two years and a student group to bring Warren Zevon to UWM, but Peter never gave up. This was the first of many shows Zevon and Peter did together.

At one point during the day, Hagar's manager asked Peter if he had a car. When Peter said he did, the manager asked him to drive Hagar around the block from the venue to the Hyatt Regency after the show in order to avoid the scrum of fans who'd be waiting by the limousine for a photo op and autograph.

That night after the show, no one noticed the trio making for the orange Mustang, but once they got in, the manager told Peter to make haste.

Peter didn't think before the line slipped out. "I can't drive fifty-five," he said.

Hagar, in the passenger seat, cringed at Peter's lame attempt to turn the title of one of his biggest hits into a punchline. In the rearview mirror, Peter caught sight of the manager's head shaking. It was dark, but he could feel the accompanying eyeroll. Four misplaced words was all it took to transform the thrill of chauffeuring one of his favorite acts into the longest short drive of Peter's life.

Later that month, Peter received a finalized contract for Batman 101. ACG would pay three thousand dollars for a forty-five-minute lecture on November 17, following a screening of the movie. West agreed to do two promotional events with WQFM in advance: a November 8 phone call with morning DJ Steve Palec to announce the show and another call a week later to be part of a dating game.

ACG also agreed to a ten-day release to Adam West for theatrical offers. If West was offered a movie or TV deal before November 7, the show would be canceled. But chances of that were slim to nil. In the 1980s, West was still at the mercy of a generation of casting directors who refused to see him as anything other than Batman. Peter paid eighty-five dollars for a copy of the movie from Films Incorporated.

In 1984, the screening of a movie from the 1960s followed by a talk back with one of its stars was unheard of, but Peter thought it would be a fun event. Based on the reviews in the *Milwaukee Journal* and *Crazy Shepherd*, he was right.
ARTWORK BY
JOHN KOMP

93 QFM   ACG

BATMAN
101 (NON-CREDIT)

FEATURING:
A SCREENING OF THE CLASSIC
'BATMAN' MOVIE
PLUS

GUEST LECTURE
ADAM WEST!

SAT. NOV. 17
8PM
UWM UNION
BALLROOM
$5 STUDENTS
$6 PUBLIC
ALL AGES WELCOME!

TICKETS AT
MAINSTREAM
RADIO DOCS
UWM BOOKSTORE
AND AT THE DOOR

INFO 963-6666

johnkomp

One unexpected expense was the result of an oversight on West and Sherrell's part. It was standard industry practice for a contract to stipulate that the promoter would be responsible for the performer's airfare and lodging, but West's contract with ACG hadn't specified that. Peter could have said no, but he didn't. The economy seat on the flight was $345, and Peter got the $45 student rate at the Marc Plaza Hotel. When West arrived at the airport, Peter was parked outside baggage claim to meet him. As West settled into the passenger seat of the Mustang, Peter seized the moment to see if he could make a car joke land better than his Sammy Hagar bomb.

"Atomic batteries to power, turbines to speed," he said. West gave an appreciative laugh as they pulled away from the curb. Peter dropped him at the hotel and arranged to return shortly after the movie started.

Back at the Ballroom, Peter made sure everything was in order. Ticket sales had been disappointing. There were some walk-ins, but not as many as he'd hoped for. About 500 people sat in the room set up to hold 750. He noticed a couple of reporters, so at least there was that.

After his event at UWM, Adam West lingered and talked with attendees who stayed to greet him, and he posed for a picture with the guy who'd gotten him there.

About thirty minutes into the movie, he left for the hotel. West was waiting; Peter skipped the Batmobile joke when he got in. After arriving at the union, they walked by a men's room on the way to the stage entrance.

West stopped. "We have time?" he asked.

"Go ahead," Peter said.

West pushed the door open, and Peter watched it slide shut behind him, thinking he probably should have priced the tickets higher. He snapped back into the moment when he saw the door swing open, but the emerging figure wasn't West. It was a student, wide-eyed, jaw hanging slack as he walked aimlessly down the hall. Catching sight of Peter, the student stopped, gathering himself, groping for words. "You are not going to believe this," he finally spat out. "I was just pissing next to Batman!"

With the end of the semester approaching, Peter's fellow students were sweating papers and exams. Peter, on the other hand, was working toward different milestones involving shows off UWM's campus. The first was in December. The others conflicted with the beginning of UWM's spring semester but also offered a once-in-a-lifetime chance to expand his range and knowledge base. No way he was going to let that kind of an opportunity pass him by.

The December show was with American guitar icon John Fahey. Peter didn't want to pass on the date he'd been offered just because there were no rooms available at UWM. It was his first experience putting on a show in a venue that wasn't associated with campus or run by another promoter. He rented a local club that would otherwise have been closed that night—Rum Doodles, which had formerly been the legendary Milwaukee venue the Jazz Gallery. Aside from this being a venue he hadn't worked before, there was nothing memorable about the show. Unless you counted the moment in the men's room. Fahey walked in with a bottle of Heineken, stood at a urinal next to Peter, and downed the entire bottle while emptying his bladder.

The show was a success—another challenge surmounted and another lesson learned. Off-campus ACG shows could draw enough people to make them a viable option. His next challenge, in January, would be a very different experience.

4

On the Road

On a Saturday night in mid-January 1985, the Christmas tree was still up in the Jests' living room. Garland lights twinkled in the windows, Sinatra crooned from the living room stereo, and four couples sat at the dining-room table playing sheepshead. It was club night, and Marvin and Kathryn were hosting.

Peter stood by the front window, watching the street. Here and there, he'd catch snippets of conversation and intermittent laughter behind him, but his main focus was what was going on outside, which so far amounted to cars driving by the house. His packed suitcase stood by the door, his winter coat hanging over it. When he saw a van, and then a station wagon, pull up and park, he pulled his coat on as he walked to the table.

"Mom," he said. Kathryn looked up. "They're here. I'll see you in two weeks."

Kathryn stood and put her hand on her husband's shoulder; Marvin got up, and they walked Peter to the door.

"Drive safely, have fun, and call if you need anything. Ten cities, right?"

"Eleven, Dad," Peter said. "I put the list on the refrigerator, so you can check where we are when."

Hugs all around, and Peter was out the door. A tall, heavy-set figure with long hair opened the back door of the van as Peter hefted his suitcase inside. From inside the van, he could see his parents watching from the window, waiting for the small caravan to pull away.

Peter was going on the road with the Violent Femmes, the Milwaukee-based punkish trio that had gone national after being plucked off a street corner in 1981. On the afternoon of August 23 of that year, before a

47

Pretenders concert in Milwaukee, James Honeyman-Scott, the band's guitarist, had stopped to listen to some musicians busking in front of the Oriental Theater. He liked what he heard enough that, on his word, bandleader Chrissie Hynde invited the trio to play an acoustic mini-set at the Pretenders' show that night, after the warm-up act and before the headliners. From there, it had been a short hop to a record deal. "Blister in the Sun," the single from the band's 1983 self-titled debut album, became a college radio hit. In early 1985, Violent Femmes weren't at the Pretenders' level, but they were on their way.

It would be Peter's first experience on the road with a band. Instead of being the promoter dealing with the tour manager and the act, Peter would be the tour manager dealing with the promoter and the venue. But it wasn't his first experience with the band—he'd promoted two Femmes shows at UWM. He'd also been in the second row for the legendary Pretenders show in 1981. With forty of his own shows under his belt, plus the ones he'd worked as a runner, Peter was pretty confident about what the job entailed. In addition to dealing with tour managers, he'd read enough contract riders to write a job description for the position.

He was already familiar with the Femmes' rider, which, among other things, detailed the band's name (Violent Femmes, no capital *The*), technical requirements (equipment, speaker systems, sound board), and specifications for lighting, sound check (time to be provided on request), load-in/load-out (one parking space close to the stage door), food and drink (one gallon orange or grapefruit juice, two large bottles of Perrier or club soda, one case of imported beer, one large pitcher of ice water, five hot meals—two vegetarian), ten clean towels, dressing rooms (a clean, secure, well-lit room that could comfortably fit six people and with a key provided to the tour manager), free tickets (only a limited number and a list of those given free tickets to be provided), photography and recording (not to be permitted), and payment (to be provided the night of the show).

Peter had done a tour manager's job booking the flights and a hotel room for Adam West. But for this tour, the Femmes' band manager, Mark Van Hecke, had taken care of transport and lodging. He'd rented a van and booked hotel rooms for stops on their way west, in Salt Lake City on the night of their first show, in the ten cities that followed (Beverly Hills, Santa Barbara, and Berkeley in California; Corvallis and Portland

Peter was twenty years old when he went on tour with the Violent Femmes in early 1985. At five feet nine inches and 130 pounds, and usually dressed in a T-shirt and jeans, he was often mistaken for a teenage runner by the acts he was promoting.

in Oregon; Vancouver, British Columbia, in Canada; Seattle, Washington; and San Francisco, San Diego, and Long Beach in California), and on the road home.

Peter had been on road trips with his family—since before he could remember they'd driven to Panama City, Florida, every Easter—but this was different. For one thing, he was on the road with guys who were of legal drinking age, something he wouldn't be for another eight months. By music business standards, Peter was a pretty straight arrow. He didn't smoke and had no interest in recreational drugs. He was a picky and very conventional eater. He'd had a girlfriend, but only one.

There were ten people on the tour: the three Femmes (Gordon Gano, Brian Ritchie, and Victor DeLorenzo); the horn section, which Ritchie had dubbed the Horns of Dilemma, consisting of Peter Balestrieri, Sigmund Snopek, and Steve Mackay; the lighting and sound guys; and Gordon's brother Glenn, who was handling merch. Gordon and Glenn drove separately in their own car; everyone else was in one of the two vehicles that composed the caravan, a station wagon and a van carrying the band's instruments and gear.

The Femmes were on the way up, but they were nowhere near the point at which they would eventually crest. Forget luxury tour buses, five-star hotels, and all the other perks that come with being a top-level rock act. This was one step up from where they'd started with four musicians and one player (Balestrieri) doubling as road manager. They had previously subsisted on a meager food allowance and slept in their van or crashed on people's floors. This run included a more generous per diem, motel rooms, and a dedicated tour manager. More food money and real beds were a good thing, but the band was incredulous when they first found out that Van Hecke had hired a twenty-year-old for the job.

When it came to the music, the Femmes always played well together. Offstage, their strong personalities didn't always mesh. They were known for being difficult with one another and with other people. Like Peter, they did not tolerate fools or foolishness, as they defined it. Unlike Peter, though, they had life experience and a collective confidence. They were also energized by performing live in front of thousands of screaming fans. For Peter, that was the stuff of bad dreams.

The initial leg was a nineteen-hour nonstop run from Milwaukee to the first gig in Salt Lake City. That ride, more Hunter S. Thompson road trip than family vacation, was the first of a slew of eye-opening new experiences for Peter. There was no formal orientation, no one explaining what to expect. Thrust into a role that would have been a challenge for anyone, he was pretty much on his own.

For musicians, touring can often be described as a road trip that combines long hours stuck in a vehicle punctuated by intermittent adrenaline rushes on stage. For Peter, however, the adrenaline rushes were constant. In the van, quietly (and sometimes not so quietly) he stewed over whether they'd be at the venue on time, wondered (always quietly) if everything would be in order when they got there, made sure all the paperwork was in order, and kept track of who needed what and when they needed it. At the motels, he made sure everyone was ready to leave on time to get to wherever they were going next.

He'd done one thing before they set out that minimized some of his anxiety. Back in Milwaukee, he'd bought a pair of walkie-talkies that plugged into a car charger. The vehicles in the caravan could be in contact to coordinate stops and each could apprise the other of anything that might come up. Who rode in which vehicle stayed loose, and everyone but Brian (who didn't have a driver's license) took turns behind the wheel. In addition to using the walkie-talkies for business, they also swapped stories to pass the time—tales of past travels, past girlfriends, and other minutiae.

Early in the tour, Brian decreed that there could not be two Peters on the same tour and, since Balestrieri had seniority, Jest would have to be called something else. Brian settled on "Shirley," a play on Peter's last name, as in "surely, you jest."

For all the light moments on the tour, and there were many, it wasn't all smooth going. Peter, a.k.a. Shirley, through no fault of his own other than being young and inexperienced, sorely tried the patience and goodwill of his more experienced travel companions. There were major clashes with Mackay, a seasoned rock-'n'-roller in his forties who'd been in the Stooges and played with Snakefinger and a host of other acts. Mackay wasn't interested in taking direction from an inexperienced kid and didn't care who knew it. It also didn't help that Van Hecke (who, after a single road tour, had refused to travel with them again) was using Peter as a conduit to tell the band anything he didn't want to say to them directly. In the midst of touring and all it entailed, DeLorenzo, Gano, and Ritchie didn't have the luxury of perspective to consider that it might be the manager and not the messenger on whom they should unleash their ire.

At the same time, Peter's passion for and obvious commitment to doing the best job he could was clear to the band members. Both DeLorenzo and Balestrieri made themselves available, answering questions and helping him with parts of the job that were new to him. They saw him as an able and willing student who did the job well, considering his limited experience.

In addition to what he was learning on the job, Peter's worldview was expanding. He was eating—and developing a fondness for—Mexican, Indian, and Thai food. He was seeing parts of the country he'd never visited, even if it was mostly out of a van window. He sent postcards to his parents from the road. Coming into Las Vegas at night, he wrote, he was struck by the beauty of the city lights. He did not write home, however, about the young woman he met at a California motel. Four different people came away from that night with four different versions of the story. She was in his room. She was not in his room. It happened in Santa Monica. It happened in Berkeley. The briefcase with the money and contracts was open and visible. The briefcase was on the desk and closed. She never knew there was a briefcase. Where everyone agreed was that Peter didn't realize she was a sex worker until he was explicitly told by his more experienced travel companions. In the end, he extricated himself from the situation with the briefcase, the money, and his virtue intact.

Like Gordon, Peter spent his postshow nights sleeping at the motel rather than partying at the bar into the wee hours with Victor, Brian, and the others. Between gigs and in the van, Peter got used to regular

When Peter began using this briefcase for concert promotion in 1982, it was standard-issue brown leather. By the time he took it on tour with the Femmes in 1985, he'd begun to informally document its history through memorabilia stuck to its exterior.

ribbing from his short-term bosses. He also made an unlikely friend. Peter was a churchgoing Christian who dreamed of having a house full of pets one day. Brian was an atheist who didn't understand why anyone would want an animal in their house. What they shared was the same abrasive sensibility—neither one had the time or inclination to sugarcoat their feelings when dealing with others. This turned out to be a good foundation on which to build a lifelong friendship.

At the end of the twenty-one-day run, as far as the band was concerned, Peter had done what he was hired to do.

"Did everybody survive? Yeah," said Balestrieri. "Did we get all the money? Yeah."

"We had fun with him," said Ritchie, "and nobody died."

For Peter, the tour had been transformative—the equivalent of successfully completing a semester abroad in a country that doesn't welcome outsiders. Yet, he returned home secure in the knowledge that he liked waking up in his own bed. Tour management was not where his future lay.

The Femmes continued to work with Peter in his capacity as a promoter, the job he loved and kept on getting better at doing. Their first posttour collaboration was a March 29, 1985, homecoming show jokingly called the Great Return, held at the Oriental Theater. The sold-out gig kicked off with the Femmes and Horns of Dilemma marching to the venue, as they played their instruments, from Victor DeLorenzo's house on Milwaukee's East Side. When they arrived at the Oriental, they entered through the front door and paraded up the center aisle of the theater and onto the stage.

Walkie-talkies played a role in that show, too, although in a different capacity than Peter had deployed them on the tour. A friend of DeLorenzo's had gotten him a pair of walkie-talkies, and the band had placed one on the sound board in the theater. As the audience sat waiting for the show to begin, more than a few people were likely wondering about the strange noises coming through the sound system. The mystery was cleared up when the band burst through the doors, marched down the aisle, and took the stage. Peter's parents, Marvin and Kathryn, were sitting in front, next to Gordon Gano's parents, who had warned them to wear earplugs. The show was a stunning success. Peter's mother remembers it this way: "We were the relatives sitting in the first or second row. It wasn't our kind of music—it was awful loud. But we were there."

Including the Great Return, ACG hosted forty-two shows in 1985. And Peter continued to audit one-credit classes, clearly prioritizing his concerts over his coursework. In the summer, he returned to Summerfest as Bob Babisch's assistant, processing all the performers' contracts, making sure everyone had parking and festival passes, and managing daily schedules that detailed who was playing when and on which stage. There was just one hiccup. At UWM, where Peter was basically at the top of the concert-promoting food chain, no one cared what he wore or how he worked. But Bo Black, Babisch's boss and the festival's executive director, was less than impressed with the new assistant's wardrobe of sloppy T-shirts and ripped jeans. Babisch was the one who delivered the message: Peter needed to dress better. A few polo shirts and some new blue jeans later, he looked presentable, if not exactly professional.

That fall, his academic responsibilities dropped to an all-time low—he audited a single one-credit class, Caves: The Underground World. At the same time, he was booking what would be some of the most important performers of his career. On October 20, ACG hosted Arlo Guthrie at the

Miller High Life Rock Series
and the Alternative Concert Group present

VIOLENT FEMMES LIVE!

FRIDAY, MARCH 29   8 P.M.
ORIENTAL THEATRE

Tickets: Oriental Theatre, UWM Bookstore,
Radio Doctors, Mainstream

ALTERNATIVE CONCERT GROUP AND
MILLER HIGH LIFE PRESENT
VIOLENT FEMMES
ORIENTAL THEATRE

0849
SEC   ROW   SEAT
GEN. ADM.
MAR 29, 1985
ADMIT ONE THIS DATE ONLY

MAR 29 1985

MILWAUKEE, WI
FRIDAY
8:00 PM

NO REFUND PRICE NO EXCHANGE
$10.00
DOOR

SEC   ROW   SEAT
GEN. ADM.
0849

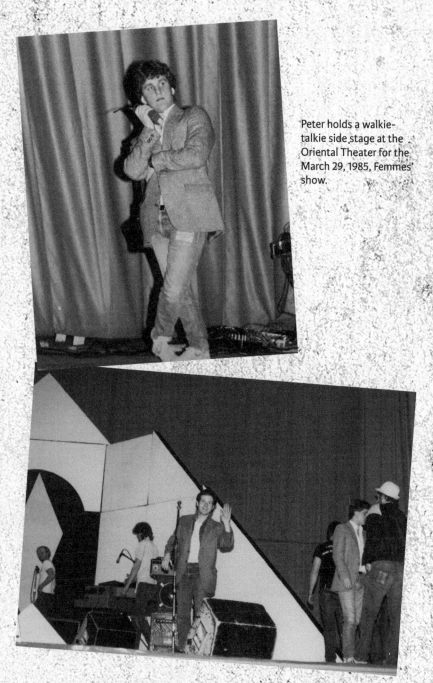

Peter holds a walkie-talkie side stage at the Oriental Theater for the March 29, 1985, Femmes' show.

Sigmund Snopek (far left), Victor DeLorenzo (center), and Peter (second from right) on stage at the Oriental on March 29.

750-seat Wisconsin Room. It was the first of more than one hundred dates Peter and Arlo would do together over the ensuing decades, becoming friends along the way. A John Prine show that month would have similar long-lasting effects. Ten years and several shows later, they embarked on a friendship that would endure until Prine's death in 2020.

5

Brushes with Stardom

Four years into his UWM promoting adventure, Peter had learned a lot about the assembly line of moving parts and the labyrinthine process of putting on a show. In the beginning, promoters like Steve Mandelman and Pat Casey had eased Peter into the process, giving him the ability to focus on what he needed to learn about the basics: pricing, logistics, and publicity. Pat had introduced him to the promoter who helped with Spyro Gyra and the Outlaws. The time Peter spent stuffing envelopes and answering phones in Steve's office before that first John Mayall show had also played a part. But at some point, Peter had picked up a copy of *Performance*, a monthly trade magazine that tracked artists' representation, who was on tour and where, who was going on tour and when, who was in the recording studio and when they might be releasing their album-in-progress, and other industry news. Within a short time, Peter had his own subscription.

When ACG first started, Peter would cold-call agents. They weren't random calls. The notebooks of data from his Milwaukee Lutheran ticket-reselling business (quantity bought, quantity resold, and profit realized) along with the notebook of the shows he attended and how they ranked (4 = excellent; 1 = below average) informed his choices. He had a sense of which acts would work in Milwaukee's market, and he had the beginnings of a reputation since booking Spyro Gyra and the Outlaws.

It also worked in his favor when agents heard "University of Wisconsin–Milwaukee" and "student group." Their lived experience of working with publicly funded state schools meant there would be no concerns as to whether their checks would clear. On the flip side, a lot could go wrong

This photo accompanied a *Milwaukee Journal* story by Jim Higgins about ACG's 1985–1986 concert season at UWM, which included shows by Arlo Guthrie, Jane Siberry, and Sun Ra.
© MILWAUKEE JOURNAL SENTINEL - USA TODAY NETWORK

with a student show, and no agent wanted to inflict unnecessary suffering on the performer they were representing.

Elizabeth Rush and Fred Bohlander were two of the first agents with whom Peter established a bond. Elizabeth's roster included the Roches, Richard Thompson, and Leon Redbone. Fred represented Leo Kottke, among others. They knew Peter was essentially a kid who didn't know what he was doing, but that didn't stop them from giving him a chance. And over time, as they watched him figure it out, they kept giving him shows.

In 1985, Elizabeth worked with Peter to bring the Roches—sisters Maggie, Terre, and Suzzy—to the Kenwood Inn for two shows in November. By June of 1986, she found herself on the phone giving Peter some last-minute instructions about Leon Redbone, who was playing a show at Century Hall, one of Peter's first at a non-UWM venue.

"Now, Leon, he's a very private person. Really," Elizabeth said. "Don't talk to him. Just leave him alone."

Peter assured her that it wouldn't be a problem. It wasn't that he wasn't excited about getting to work with Leon Redbone. He was—very much so. He'd been a fan since seeing Redbone's first performance on *Saturday Night Live* in 1976. But Peter would never have shared that, even without Elizabeth's advisory warning. Leon would get the same treatment as Peter's other touring artists: a cordial welcome, an orientation to the performance space and dressing room, and information on where to find him if anything else was wanted or needed. After that, he'd make himself scarce.

On June 18, Redbone arrived, did what he did, and left. A brilliant guitarist and singer, he was a raconteur with wicked comic timing, both onstage and off, and a preternatural gift for communicating his love of Tin Pan Alley–era classics. A Redbone show was like Vaudeville for late-twentieth-century listeners. The only conversation between him and Peter concerned chairs. After arriving at the venue, Redbone walked through rooms, sitting in every chair he could find before choosing one that suited him. Over the next few years, he continued to return to Wisconsin for shows. Each time, Peter did what he'd done the time before—he stayed quiet and out of the way. And then, out of nowhere before a show at the Barrymore in Madison, Redbone initiated a conversation about the brilliance of an obscure 1930s musical act. Peter had no idea who he was talking about but somehow managed to hold up his end of the conversation well enough that it led, ultimately, to friendship.

Of course, not every act became a close friend. Some became material for great stories about missed opportunities that Peter was okay missing. One such story involved a young, little-known comedian Rush was representing named Sam Kinison. "You have got to book him," she told Peter.

Between the time Peter booked him and the night of the two shows he performed in Milwaukee, Kinison had become a hot ticket. Both shows were sellouts. Postshow, he and his tour manager invited Peter to drive to Chicago with them and party with adult film star Seka.

"No thanks," Peter told them, before heading home to eat pizza and watch *Green Acres* reruns. It was a variation on his postshow routine.

In the interval between Peter's booking and this November 1986 show, Sam Kinison had gone from a relatively unknown act to a big name.

Generally, other ACG members were around to help with load-in, load-out, and general stage crew duties. Once all postshow work was over, they'd meet up at Pizza Man on North Farwell Avenue, where Peter would treat everyone to beer and pizza. The evening of the Kinison show, Peter had been able to handle the final tasks of the night—settling up with the act and passing on the porn star party—on his own.

By 1987, ACG was promoting as many shows outside of UWM as it was inside. That year, the group brought Bonnie Raitt to the newly opened Avalon Theater. The following week, when blues legend John Lee Hooker played at Club New York, Peter picked him up at the airport. The 1978 orange T-top Mustang he'd bought at the gas station was reliable, ran well, and was fine for anything Peter and his friends wanted to get themselves up to. But it didn't work for chauffeuring music industry professionals around the city. "Adult-in-progress" wasn't the image he wanted to project to artists and their financiers, especially a venerable performer

This family shot—featuring (left to right) Jonathan, Peter, Marvin, Karen, and Timothy Jest—taken in the mid-1980s, shows why it was easy for an act to assume Peter was a low-level staffer, rather than a promoter.

like Hooker. Peter couldn't change his age or looks—at twenty-two, he was still occasionally mistaken for a high schooler. His solution was to regularly deploy a tactic out of a high schooler's playbook, one that worked in his favor: he'd borrow his parents' car.

The car was a perk of Marvin's job. Every three years, Auer Steel & Heating would replace the previous General Motors model with something newer—sometimes an Oldsmobile Cutlass, sometimes a Buick Electra. Marvin was as meticulous about his car's appearance and upkeep as he was supportive of his youngest son's burgeoning career. As a result, Peter always had something sharp to drive when the occasion called for it. He'd pick up the artist and sometimes a manager or other member of the touring ensemble and drop them at their hotel in advance of the gig. Sometimes they assumed he was the runner or someone hired to drive.

At the luggage carousel, Peter spotted Hooker, who was traveling with his bass player and road manager. The road manager carried the luggage to the car, handing it off for Peter to put in the trunk before sliding into the front passenger seat. Peter held the back driver's-side door open for Hooker; the bass player placed his instrument in the center seat before settling in behind the road manager. The car was silent as Peter pulled away from the airport. For Hooker, being picked up at the airport was just another day at the office. Peter was chatting with the road manager about the gig when a voice piped up from the back seat.

"You're the promoter?" Hooker said, his Southern drawl tinged with surprise. "Why, you're just a kid!"

It wasn't the first time an artist had expressed that sentiment, but Hooker was more impressed than taken aback by Peter's youth. Peter took it as a compliment. He was generally fine with musicians not realizing who he was as he drove them to the hotel or venue. Too many artists— and certainly too many managers—got squirrelly when they met him, assuming that he couldn't possibly know what he was doing. Some even thought they should settle up before the gig; otherwise, they might not get paid. But Peter did know what he was doing, and he was becoming more confident with every show he successfully pulled off. Though he couldn't have seen it coming, an event was about to occur that would take his career to a new level.

In April of 1988, one of the city's most popular clubs, Century Hall, burned down. The fire had spread from Farwell Avenue's Fox Bay building, which housed a paint and wallpaper shop with apartments above it. Century Hall, next door, had started its life as a tobacco warehouse a hundred years earlier, and it had been combined with another building sometime in the early 1920s to become a single, large space. In the 1970s, after decades of neglect, it was rehabbed and became a beloved Milwaukee venue. The club hadn't been open the night the fire broke out, but a dozen residents of the Fox Bay building were injured, one seriously, and twenty-eight people were left homeless. It took 165 firefighters five hours to get the fire under control. In late July, the local head of the Bureau of Alcohol, Tobacco, and Firearms announced that the cause was arson.

Peter had done several shows at Century Hall. Its permanent closure and the subsequent decision by the building's owners to replace it with a strip mall left a hole in Milwaukee's club scene. He'd also done shows at other clubs, like the Toad and the Odd Rock. The Funny Bone comedy club, which had formerly been the Barn and then Teddy's, was just a couple of miles down the street from Century Hall. Peter had booked one ACG show at the Funny Bone—the New Age performer Scott Cossu—on a night when the UWM Union rooms were full and the club was available.

He also had enough connections by then to be getting calls from agents with acts looking for venues. Still, there were plenty of acts who didn't need to reach out, acts who could announce their availability to tour, then sit back and wait while promoters in multiple cities fought for a handful of dates. These acts, for the most part, dealt only with the major promoters in each market, so they didn't seek out offers from smaller promoters. Roughly a dozen agencies throughout the country, with representatives in each region, were the points of contact for promoters looking to book with a professional touring act.

Iggy Pop was one act that Peter had been keeping his eye on. In 1988, about a week after finding out that the Century Hall fire had been arson, Peter learned that Iggy would play a series of Midwestern dates on his *Instinct* tour. A fan since Iggy's mid-1970s collaborations with David Bowie, Peter didn't have to think twice about breaking his rule about booking an act just because he wanted to see it. He knew an Iggy Pop show in Milwaukee would sell out if he could just get a date.

On August 4, he faxed an offer to Lance Tendler, the Midwestern contact for Iggy's agency: $7,500 for Iggy to play the UWM Ballroom. Tendler was the club date contact—part of his role as assistant to Bobby Brooks, who was in charge of the Midwest territory at Creative Arts Agency (CAA). A few days later, Peter sent an additional offer, this time for a package deal with Iggy and the Ramones. For the next week, he followed up with regular phone calls. When Tendler told him the package deal was off the table, Peter reiterated his interest in a solo show. But he was uncertain about his ability to land the show, as the Riverside Theater, a much bigger venue, had also submitted an offer.

On the morning of Friday, August 26, he got a call. The show was his if he could come up with an additional five hundred dollars. Peter agreed on the condition that the date of the show be moved back a day, from a Monday to a Sunday. After some back-and-forth between the agent and Iggy's management, Peter got phone confirmation. Tendler collected all the contract information he needed to draw up the paperwork and told Peter to "go with it."

For weeks, the local music community had been abuzz with the rumor of a possible Iggy Pop show in Milwaukee. Iggy's local fans were on alert. Record-store clerks, disc jockeys, and music writers were waiting to hear, and all Peter had been able to offer was the promise that when he knew more, they would, too.

As soon as he heard "go with it," he did. Immediately after hanging up with Tendler, with the phone still to his ear, Peter dialed Paul Host, the music director at WMSE, Milwaukee's college radio station. Within the hour, word of the impending show was spreading throughout the music community.

Then, late in the afternoon, the phone rang. It was Tendler, rescinding the confirmation.

Peter hung up, reached for his inhaler, and tried to figure out his next move. Over the years, he'd managed to put out his share of sporadic show-related fires—artists taking wrong turns and showing up late, undersold shows requiring him to empty his bank account to pay the act, even process servers showing up to serve a musician paternity-suit papers before the show. But those had all occurred within the context of there actually being a show for Peter to crisis-manage. This was different. What he did next would also have to be different.

In any work situation, an employee going over their boss's head is a big deal. Peter didn't have a boss, but there was a hierarchy in the concert world. It would be a big no-no for a promoter to jump the agent and reach out to an act's manager. But this agent had pulled back the date after giving his word, violating an unspoken but widely understood norm and tearing a hole in Peter's most precious asset—his reputation. From where Peter sat, the decision to pull the show was an act of war.

Peter slipped a sheet of Alternative Concert Group stationery between the rollers and began typing. He sent the letter, via fax, to Iggy's manager, Art Collins, and copied the CAA agents. In two pages, he outlined the situation:

Bobby Brooks . . . informed me that he did not know that [his assistant had] confirmed my date, because he confirmed a Madison show on September 26. Playing the Milwaukee date would mean that Iggy would be playing eight straight days, which was something he could not do. I informed Bobby that I had already announced the show and that people were very excited. After waiting for ten years, and hearing rumors that Iggy would finally be coming to Milwaukee, the buzz in town was very strong. I asked Bobby to please talk to Rob Light, Lance, Art Collins, and Barry Taylor, to see if [there] is any way possible we could still do the show on September 25, 1988.

If it comes down to it, I feel a play for $8,000 in Milwaukee, where he hasn't played in 10 years, is better than a club date in Madison, where he has performed many times.

Saturday came and went with no news. On Sunday, he got a call from a friend in Madison, who dished some juicy intel about Iggy Pop's Madison show—the proposed venue had changed. A Milwaukee concert had never been announced publicly, but Peter knew, based on his single call to Paul Host at WMSE, that it was only a matter of time before people would be looking to buy tickets. Peter needed answers.

Monday came and went with no news.

On Tuesday, he faxed another letter:

Lance Tendler informed me that [there] was still no date for me. They would rather play Madison. Yesterday, [the] Madison [show] was moved from Headliners because they wanted to show Monday Night Football! CAA now says the [Madison] date is set at the Union Theater but according to the director . . . they cannot confirm it until the students meet next week. He also said they really do not want to do it but the promoter is in a spot.

Why does CAA want to play Iggy Pop in a town where no venue wants to do him? Especially when the much bigger town of Milwaukee is starving for an Iggy Pop show. I am still holding September 25, 26 at the UWM Ballroom and my $8,000 offer is still good. Please let me know if we can work this out.

The next day, he got a call from Brooks, who delivered the news, a blast of icy rage in a single sentence: "You went over my head, but you got your fucking date," he told Peter. "You'd better do well."

He did. Thor Christensen, the *Milwaukee Journal*'s music critic, wrote that Iggy Pop, backed by a "brash but well-oiled quartet . . . raised hell Sunday night in the sweaty, sold-out ballroom of the University of Wisconsin–Milwaukee Union[,] covering the stage like a welterweight boxer gone berserk."

As usual, Peter stayed in the background throughout the day of the show, while making sure everything was running well. Then, at the end of the night, he introduced himself.

"You're the promoter?" Iggy asked. He cocked his head and eyeballed Peter. It was a study in contrasts: the geeky twenty-three-year-old in a Three Stooges T-shirt, baggy jeans, and sneakers and the freshly toweled-off rock legend, still dressed in the leather vest and tight jeans he'd worn on stage.

Iggy took a drink from the liter bottle of wine he was holding. Peter was holding a can of root beer. The two walked toward the band's tour bus. "So, you're a student here?" Iggy asked.

"Not really," Peter said. "I just take bowling and weather maps so I can do concerts." Since his early teens, Peter had been listening to Iggy Pop sing, but this was the first time he'd ever heard the man laugh. The sound echoed down the empty hallway as they made their way toward the exit, sweeter than anything Peter had heard on a record.

As they passed a student walking in the opposite direction, Iggy addressed him without breaking stride. "Hey!" he called out. "Hey! Do you go here? Do you take bowling, too?" The refrain was repeated every time they encountered another person until they reached the bus. "Bowling!" Iggy said, shaking his head. He took another swig from the bottle in one hand as he offered the other to Peter. "Thanks, man!"

"Thank you," Peter responded.

Iggy Pop looked Peter over once more, then turned toward the open door. He was still laughing as he stepped onto the bus.

The rest of Peter's semester was busy, with a full roster of shows both on and off campus. ACG's concerts were going well, but Peter knew that continuing to audit courses just to helm a student group was an unsustainable business model. He'd known it for a while, but it was during bowling class, as he recalled Iggy Pop's laughter while watching his ball sail toward a rack of pins, that the truth revealed itself. Peter needed his own club.

6

Welcome to the Club

There's a big difference between renting a house and buying one. When you rent, you sign a lease, put down a security deposit, pay your rent when it's due, clean up when you leave, and get your security deposit back if everything is left in order.

Buying a house isn't just a next-level proposition. It's jumping multiple rungs up a ladder. Instead of a small sum for a security deposit and first month's rent, you need a down payment—a significantly larger sum. You need to have a high enough credit rating to be approved for a bank loan. You need to understand mortgage interest rates and types and what an inspection and appraisal entail. You need to be able to make an offer, negotiate terms, know when and whether to hire an attorney, and what to do at closing.

For Peter, promoting shows at UWM and leasing out clubs for one-nighters was like renting an apartment. Opening a club would be like buying a house. Still, once the idea had settled into Peter's head, it made itself comfortable. It wasn't something he'd initially wanted to do, but the reality of the situation was that if he was going to keep doing the job he wanted to do—promote shows, help emerging artists grow their careers, and eventually promote major acts—he needed a reliable venue where he could book them.

The trajectory of a successful band from a midsized city usually goes something like this: When you're starting out, you mostly play in the back rooms of bars. Your crowd might be five people or it might be thirty. Most of them are your friends. After a while, if word gets out, you might attract a following of a hundred at your shows. Now, you get a regular blurb in the alternative weekly and maybe an invitation to be the opening act for a bigger band. From there, you might move up to headlining two-hundred-to five-hundred-seat venues, and from there, ones that seat one thousand to twenty-five hundred people. Thousands of successful artists spend their careers playing venues in that range. The few who outgrow a twenty-five-hundred-seat hall are the ones who go on to play arenas.

Most of Peter's shows fell within the three-hundred- to twelve-hundred-person range. He imagined the club he owned would be at the lower end of that spectrum. The reasons were simple and twofold. For one thing, a smaller club would cost less to run. For another, the loss of two clubs of that size—Club New York and Century Hall—in less than a year had left a gap in Milwaukee's live-music landscape. He could easily step into that gap. If, that is, he could find a venue, gather enough money, and jump through all the regulatory and logistical hoops.

Over on Milwaukee's near-south side, Jack Koshick owned the Odd Rock Café. The club, which featured mostly rock and punk acts, had gained national attention in March of 1989 when punk rocker GG Allin was arrested there for defecating on stage and throwing fecal matter at the audience during his set. He'd been doing it onstage since 1985 but, until that point, had not done so in Milwaukee. Koshick stopped the show. Allin was fined $1,000 and sentenced to ninety days in prison, and a warrant was issued for his arrest. In response, Allin wrote and recorded "Shove That Warrant Up Your Ass."

Peter and Jack had teamed up to copromote a handful of shows, including Primus and Fishbone, at the Eagles Club. They had casually batted around the idea of opening up a club together, but it had never gone any further. Then, on New Year's Eve of 1988, the Funny Bone went out of business. The club at 1434 North Farwell Avenue had had a long run as Teddy's. Its owner, Tony Machi, a denizen of Milwaukee's Italian community, had named it after his son. In 1984, nervous about the future of his business when the drinking age in Wisconsin climbed from eighteen to nineteen and then to twenty-one, he made the decision to close Teddy's and extended a long-term lease to the comedy club chain. Now the Funny Bone was gone, too.

As Teddy's, the building had been one of the city's leading rock clubs, hosting acts like John Lee Hooker, Black Flag, and the Oil Tasters. Before that, the century-old building had functioned as a garage and storage

facility. But its musical roots predated live
shows. From 1947 to 1965, 1434 North
Farwell Avenue was the Wisconsin dis-
tribution center for Capitol Records.
Three years after Capitol vacated, Machi
had opened the Barn, the building's first
incarnation as a live-music venue. By
1973, after a fire and a renovation, the
club was operating as Teddy's.

Now, in 1989, Peter was thinking the
former Teddy's could be the location of
his new club. He went to see Jack about
partnering to co-own the club. It would
be an opportunity for Jack to expand
his reach beyond the near-south side
and get a foothold in a different part
of town. His presence at the Odd Rock
wouldn't be compromised because
Peter would be the point person at
the new place. Jack had the day-to-
day experience of running a club that
Peter didn't; Peter had the know-how
and relationships with agents and

By 1989, Peter had worked
at Summerfest for five consecutive
years and was manager of the
"Leiny's" stage.

managers to attract a wide array of new and established talent beyond
Jack's existing connections. Most of all, the arrangement would give Peter
what he really needed: his own base of operations where he could help
build up developing acts. As Peter knew from firsthand experience, it was
possible to book an act like Pearl Jam for $1,000 in a 270-seat club. In
theory, if they liked what you did, you could continue working with them
as they moved up the music business food chain until you were promoting
them in a 20,000-seat arena like Milwaukee's Bradley Center or a 41,900-
seat spot like Miller Park.

At twenty-four, Peter had learned enough about the music business
in Milwaukee to see Jack as someone who would make a good business
partner. Some club owners were all business, and some were in it for the
parties, but Jack genuinely liked the music. Peter knew that quality was

A view of Shank Hall's interior, circa 1990.

relatively rare, and he recognized it as something they had in common. As co-owners, he imagined they would both book talent, while Peter would take the lead on business-related issues and navigating the new aspects of owning his own venue.

What neither of them had was a lot of money. Jack had a friend—his bouncer—who was also interested in getting into the club business. They invited him into the mix. That spring, the three put their heads together and, based on what they knew of the neighborhood, the condition of the building, and what was involved in opening costs, agreed that they would each put in $10,000 by September.

Peter would be in charge of legwork. He called Bob Weidenbaum, a lawyer he'd met while working with the promoter Pat Casey. Bob, a music fan, had become a friend and occasional adviser. Peter knew he was the person to handle the lease, partnership, and incorporation paperwork.

Next, he set up a meeting with Jim Wiechmann, who owned the building. On their own, none of the three partners was credit-worthy enough to sign a lease. After dinner one night, Peter asked his father if he'd be willing to cosign. Marvin and Kathryn, who had spent many years watching their son build something out of nothing, said yes immediately. The trio set a September 5 date to have their money in order and form a corporation. In June, Peter and Marvin signed a five-year lease that would start October 1. In the interim, he and Jack partnered up to bring the Red Hot Chili Peppers to Madison and Green Bay later in the year.

On September 5, Peter had his money ready. Jack and the bouncer didn't—and, as it turned out, wouldn't. Peter had been checking in with Jack periodically to make sure everything was still on track with the money as the September 5 date approached. Every time, Jack had assured him that things were fine. But on September 4, when Peter called to firm things up for the meeting where they'd actually put their names on the paperwork, Jack asked for an extension. Peter said no. He'd given Jack the benefit of the doubt. That they'd violated the first commandment of business—reneging after pledging that they'd make the long-agreed-upon deadline—was bad enough. But blown trust wasn't the worst of it.

Every member of Peter's family went to work, came home, and, every two weeks, received a paycheck. Every member of Peter's family had a retirement account and a savings account and knew exactly how much money they would be getting when. Marvin had signed a legal agreement based on Peter's trust. Peter had trusted that Jack and the bouncer would do what they said they would do. Now, the whole thing was falling apart.

"What kind of idiots do this?" Peter asked, pacing back and forth in Bob Weidenbaum's law office. "My dad's retirement is on the line, and it's my fault."

Bob sat at his desk, watching Peter. He listened, occasionally glancing at his watch, then looking back up at wherever Peter was in the loop between the office door and the window. Then, as Peter paused to catch his breath before launching into another segment of his tirade, Bob spoke. He didn't ask whether Peter had his share of the money, because he already knew the answer.

"You were supposed to sign articles of incorporation," he said.

Peter turned toward the desk, aiming something between a stare and a glare at Bob. "I know I'm supposed to sign articles of incorporation. That's why I'm here with my money! I keep my promises! Those idiots! I can't believe this."

Bob's hand was curled beneath his chin, his pointer finger tapping against the side of his mouth, and his eyebrows furrowed. As Peter paused to take a breath, he glanced over and caught Bob's expression. It was the same look he'd seen on some of his solo acts before they took the stage, and it brought him up short. Reflexively, he knew the proper thing to do. He stood, quiet. He waited. The silence was strangely soothing. Then, Bob spoke.

"You know?" he said. "It could be good to co-own a club."

Peter's eyes narrowed as he took in what Bob was saying. He cocked his head at the lawyer. "Are you saying what I think you're saying?"

"I am if you can come up with $15,000," he said. "We'll be 50 percent partners."

After Peter scraped the extra $5,000 together from his savings, hurdle one had been surmounted. Next up were the articles of incorporation, which Bob set to work creating. He also applied for licenses, which required approval from the Milwaukee Common Council. They would need two: one for entertainment and one for liquor. But before Bob could even submit the liquor license application, an issue had to be resolved. Back in 1984, Alternative Concert Group had approached Miller Brewing Company about sponsoring its shows. Miller worked that aspect of its business through a local marketing company, GMR. Each year, Peter would tell GMR how many shows he was planning on doing and ask for a specific amount of money. In 1984, it had been $3,000. In exchange, he would send GMR all the advertising and other promotional media featuring Miller's name and logo that he created for each show, in order to verify that he was keeping his side of the agreement. He also provided GMR with ten complimentary tickets to each show.

The sponsorship provided more than money, not that the money didn't matter. It also added a layer of legitimacy to ACG—it helped allay concerns anyone might have about getting into bed, business-wise, with a guy barely old enough to drink legally. And it also came with a serious perk. Once a month, a Miller truck would roll up to wherever Peter was living—first his parents' house, then the apartment he shared with Mike Wallander, and then eventually his own place—and deliver ten cases of Miller High Life in glass bottles.

To Peter's mind, that was the best part of the deal. Since most of his acts were soloists or small ensembles, ten cases a month basically amounted to an endless supply of free beer. At UWM, where most of his shows occurred, a promoter bringing in his own alcohol would have been grounds for all kinds of trouble. Nonetheless, after load-out, the sponsorship brew would always materialize.

Any university official wandering around backstage would have spotted the food and drink laid out for the artist and crew and passed by without giving it a second glance. Peter always put in a requisition from union catering that included food and drinks. The beer on the table was a red herring, though. He would order one six-pack of Miller from the caterers and keep replenishing it from the complimentary Miller cases. To the casual observer, it was six bottles of beer that lasted forever. In all the years ACG did shows at UWM, no one ever raised a question about the Miracle of the Endless Six-Pack. It might have been different if the shows weren't generating revenue on bar sales from his audiences. But they always did.

The sponsorship also allowed Peter to occasionally procure complimentary tickets to Bucks and Brewers games. The downside was that it rendered Peter ineligible to apply for a liquor license. When Jack and Mark had been on board, Peter hadn't worried. They didn't have the same conflicts. But things were different now. He needed to find an agent, someone to apply for Shank Hall's license. It had to be someone he trusted absolutely and someone who trusted him, too. If something ever happened, this person would have to feel secure in the knowledge that Peter would do what was necessary to shield them from liability.

Bob would have been the most logical choice, but he lived in the suburbs, and the agent had to be a city resident. Peter asked Mike Stefaniak, a friend who tended bar at LA Freeway, about a mile north and west of Shank Hall on the corner of North and Oakland Avenues. They knew each other from being on opposite sides of the bar, but they were also connected through the local music scene. Mike was a singer-songwriter and guitarist, and Peter had booked both his former band (Umbrella Man) and current band (Arms and Legs and Feet) for Summerfest in years past. Also, Bob had done some legal work for Arms and Legs and Feet. Like Peter, Mike was young—twenty-six to Peter's twenty-four—single, and savvy. He was smart enough to say yes when he saw an opportunity to benefit his band by doing a favor for someone else.

Agreeing to be the agent for Shank's liquor license meant Mike would have a serious in with the owners of a local venue. What none of them realized was that they were also inadvertently signing on as cast members in the 1989 equivalent of a one-episode reality show called "Great Moments in Bureaucracy."

After Bob submitted the license applications in September, he learned they'd be on the agenda at an October meeting of the License Committee. Alderwoman Larraine McNamara-McGraw, a committee member who represented the district where the club would be located, immediately made her opposition known. Teddy's clubgoers had been a headache for the neighborhood, and McNamara-McGraw wasn't pleased by the prospect of a new set of old problems moving into the space. After verbally informing Bob of her stance, she mailed a postcard to every resident within a six-block radius of the club. Along with notification of Peter's intent to open the club, it listed the time, date, and location of the committee meeting and urged recipients to attend, provide public comment, and call her with questions or concerns.

Meanwhile, Bob met with Peter and Mike. They would need at least three affirmative votes from the five people on the committee to be approved for the entertainment and liquor licenses. McNamara-McGraw's opposition, Bob told Peter, was the kiss of death. It was an unwritten but generally prevailing rule that council members supported the view of the district representative. McNamara-McGraw's postcards had made it clear where she stood. The other members—Annette Scherbert, Donald Richard, and Chris Krajniak—would likely follow her lead. Committee Chair Tom Nardelli was their best and only hope, Bob said. If they could convince him, he might be able to sway the others.

Mike wanted to know what kinds of questions to expect. Bob reassured him. "Don't worry, I'll be able to answer most of the questions," he said, adding, "They probably won't ask you much specifically, and I'll handle the legal stuff or any of the harder questions." Peter just listened. He knew the best thing he could do was keep his mouth shut and let Bob speak for him.

In late October, the three of them stood in the hallway outside of Committee Room B. Mike had pulled his long hair back into a neat ponytail. Both he and Peter were wearing suit jackets; Bob looked every bit the lawyer he was.

Peter nodded hello to the cluster of their supporters—mostly local musicians and friends—who'd shown up, filing in after them and taking seats on the side of the room where he, Mike, and Bob would sit at a table, facing the committee. Bob took the middle seat. They'd all noted the group that had been on the other side of the hallway—ostensibly people from the neighborhood, along with a couple of musicians Peter hadn't expected, Bill Stace and Patrick Nedobeck.

After Nardelli read their names, Bob spoke first, describing Peter as a lifelong city resident, touting his experience and enthusiasm and their commitment to running a responsible establishment. When Teddy's was operating, the drinking age had been eighteen. Now it was twenty-one. That alone would set Shank Hall apart from its predecessor in terms of drawing a more responsible clientele. He pointed out that a vacant building wasn't going to add anything to the tax base and that Peter's goal was to build a stable, long-term business and be an asset to the neighborhood and the city.

Nardelli asked McNamara-McGraw whether she supported the license application. Holding a sheaf of stapled papers she'd removed from a folder, she began listing the responses she'd received to her postcard campaign, all in opposition.

"Are those respondents here?" Nardelli asked, pointing to the small crowd at the back of the room.

"No," McNamara-McGraw said, "but . . ."

Nardelli held his hand up to stop her. "That's inadmissible," he said. He turned to the rest of the committee. "Do you have questions?"

They did. When they asked Mike how he'd prevent minors from getting in and drinking, Bob jumped in. He reiterated that the drinking age was now twenty-one and older and that the rowdy concertgoers roaming the neighborhood who had been vividly conjured by Alderwoman McNamara-McGraw would not materialize. Bob fielded committee members' questions about the day-to-day operations. Nardelli nodded. Then he looked at the crowd. "Does anyone here have anything to say?"

A line formed as people rose to speak. Neighborhood residents expressed concerns about noise and litter. One resident complained about the night Teddy's patrons had urinated in her bushes. Bob responded to each concern, mostly by uttering variations on a single message:

Shank Hall was a new establishment with a new owner and would be a respectful neighbor. When a resident who lived six blocks away voiced concerns about how Shank would affect the neighborhood, Bob asked how much she'd been affected by Teddy's. She said she'd never noticed it.

The people who spoke in favor of Shank Hall talked about the benefits of having another local live-music venue. Some who had helped Peter with concerts at UWM spoke to his experience in putting on shows. Many musicians talked about how a new venue would improve Milwaukee's music scene.

Then Bill Stace and Pat Nedobeck got up. Stace spoke first. "Peter Jest is an abusive jerk," he said, "and you shouldn't give him a license. He doesn't know what he's doing."

Peter froze, then turned, still sitting, to face his detractors. Nedobeck's statement was a variation on Stace's theme. Peter was a bad promoter, and there was no way his club would succeed. Peter wasn't surprised to hear Stace criticize him. They'd been at odds since Stace had attempted to get his band, Three on Fire, into a festival by doing an end-run around Peter, who was in charge of securing talent for the event. Peter's response had been to refuse Three on Fire a slot during the three-day festival in down-town Milwaukee. That Stace had taken the time—and brought a friend—to denounce Peter in public? That was unexpected.

Bob placed his hand on Peter's arm, stilling him as he looked first at Stace and Nedobeck, then at Nardelli and the rest of the committee. "Peter's reputation speaks for itself," he said. "The last time I checked, being popular wasn't a requirement for obtaining a liquor license. Nor is the eventual success or failure of the venue applying for that license."

When it was over, the vote was 3-2 in favor of granting the licenses. The full Common Council would meet later in the week, but that was basically a rubber stamp. Shank Hall was a go.

7

The Music and the Mileage

Peter sat at his desk—which he'd recently relocated from his parents' basement to his office at the club he now owned—filling in his 1990 calendar. On the other side of the closed door, he heard hammering and chatter. The crew he'd hired to tear out the stage on the south wall and build a new one on the east wall, directly opposite the club's entrance, was hard at work. When they were done, he'd be able to watch shows from his office chair. Peter's vision for Shank Hall was simple. His club would be a place to grow new talent and showcase local acts. Meanwhile, ACG would continue as its own separate entity—no longer a student group but a standalone business owned by Peter that produced and promoted shows at larger venues.

The stage builders were also removing the hanging glass rack from above the bar. Since the years when the club had belonged to Tony Machi, the law had changed. The rack had become a no-no—supposedly cigarette smoke lingered there. Peter was fine with the change; removing the hanging glasses would make for better sightlines between the bar, just inside the entrance, and the newly installed stage at the back.

It was an open secret that Machi had spoken to Tom Nardelli, chair of the License Committee, the day before the committee voted to approve the license requests for Shank Hall. Peter was grateful that Machi had put in a kind word. Still, when he had time to think about it, he seethed over the full Common Council's vote. It should have been unanimous. And it would have been, but for Larraine McNamara-McGraw, who had requested that her opposition be noted in the minutes.

For now, though, time for outrage was a luxury Peter couldn't afford. It was October 24, 1989. With ten days between the final approval and Shank Hall's grand opening on November 3, every minute of his waking hours was taken up by the large and small details of opening a club. There was liquor to buy, a stage to build, staff to hire, and supplies to order. Prior to the committee meeting, Peter had made a deal with Tony Machi to acquire the existing tables, chairs, and other fixtures with the understanding that if approval didn't happen, the deal would be off. He'd booked two of his favorite local bands for opening weekend: Java, a reggae-flavored pop band out of Madison, and Semi-Twang, a local cowpunk band that had been signed by Warner Records. Semi-Twang was Peter's first choice; Java was Bob's. Peter also booked a full roster of shows into early December with the understanding that he could move them to other venues if the club didn't become a reality. For the same reason, he hadn't done any advertising or booked anything at Shank Hall beyond the end of the year.

There was no time to waste. In addition to ad buys, he was fielding calls from local news outlets who'd been reporting on the club's potential opening since early August. Talking with reporters was part of the gig. Most were supportive and excited about the new club. The *Shepherd Express*, the city's biggest alternative weekly, reported on the forthcoming opening. So did both daily papers, the *Milwaukee Journal* and the *Milwaukee Sentinel*. Then came a request from the *UWM Times*. Given that Peter was still technically a student—enrolled in a one-credit bowling class and a two-credit class called the Concert Experience—and also president of a student group, he wasn't entirely surprised by the ask.

A few days later, he and the *UWM Times* reporter sat in his office. She was asking all the usual questions—how had he gotten the idea (he told her), what kinds of acts would he be booking (he gave her the flyer), how many people could the club accommodate (240). Then came the surprise question. "Is it true," she asked, "that you used segregated fee money from your UWM student group to finance your club?"

Peter's feet were answering the question before he had a chance to formulate a single word, much less any kind of coherent sentence. He was out of his chair, walking toward his office door. "Follow me," he said. The reporter, notebook open and pen in hand, trailed behind him as he headed through the club and toward the exit door. He opened it. Light poured into the darkened venue as he turned to face the reporter, who stood waiting for Peter to answer her question.

"This interview is over," he said.

"But I heard . . ."

His left hand grasped the door handle. His right arm extended away from his body, ending in a curled fist with an index finger pointing toward the street. "Get out."

The reporter dashed from the club, stuffing the pad and pen into her bag as she hurried out.

Peter stomped back to his office. Seven years of producing shows at UWM, and that's what he got? How many times had anyone brought a national act to campus before ACG? How many hundreds of shows had he made happen there? Did people think every one was paid for with segregated fees? Peter knew there was no crossover between Alternative Concert Group and Shank Hall—they were completely separate entities. He wasn't worried about anything legal; he kept records, and there was a paper trail. But the idea that anyone suspected him of using student fees to run his new privately owned business, and the fact that a reporter would ask the question to his face, rankled him.

In the last days of October, Peter found himself staring at the stage of his new club. Inside of a week, it would begin to be occupied night after night by a range of performers. The room, he hoped, would regularly fill to capacity, with people showing up for as many shows as he could bring in. He didn't have time to waste stewing about haters and speculators. He had a club to open.

For the staff, he'd leveraged his existing connections and reached out to contacts and friends to put together a team he could trust. From UWM, he hired away Mo, the head of bar service, to manage Shank's bar. Mo hired Tracy Roe, one of his UWM bartenders, to work alongside him. Peter called Terry Cullen, whom he had first encountered back in 1982 and had subsequently hired to do various ACG events, to get advice about security. For sound and tech, Peter used the same company he'd been contracting with for his ACG shows at UWM.

An opening-week flyer, featuring the eight acts performing between November 3 and November 11, was already circulating through town. In addition to Java and Semi-Twang on the weekend, Peter had booked

New Age pianist Jim Chappel for a free show on Sunday. Monday's act was a local outfit called the Has Beens of Rock, featuring Sigmund Snopek, that had a regular Sunday gig at a bar called Harpo's. Admission was one dollar. The rest of opening week included shows by punk legend Exene Cervenka, who was touring with British folk-punk group the Oyster Band, and local guitarist Daryl Stuermer, who, in addition to his own solo work, had been part of Genesis since 1978.

The flyer featured two other bits of information. One was a laundry list of the acts coming to Shank for the rest of the month, including Leon Redbone, Shawn Colvin, Syd Straw, and the a cappella group New York Voices. There was also a short letter. "Welcome to Shank Hall!" it began.

> We at Shank Hall would like to thank everyone involved in getting us open. We have spent thousands of dollars improving the club to make it more enjoyable for playing and viewing live music. Our goal is to provide a great place for local bands to play and a great place to see local and national acts. I would like to hear from anyone with ideas, suggestions or comments on Shank Hall. Milwaukee musicians and music lovers can expect a great five years at Shank Hall. Welcome to Shank Hall and TAP INTO MILWAUKEE!

It was signed "Peter Jest, President, Shank Hall, Inc." The five years referred to the length of the lease Peter and his father had signed for the building—Peter didn't want to make any guarantees that it would stay open longer than that, in case things didn't work out. If they did, the club would stay open longer. If they didn't, Peter, who would still be just thirty when the lease expired, planned to keep promoting acts at other venues.

Milwaukee Journal reporter Tina Maples summed up the excitement of the area's music fans in a preview of the club published on opening day. "With a dwindling number of music clubs elsewhere in the city, it's little wonder that the local music community has long anticipated tonight's opening of Shank Hall, a new live music club at 1434 N. Farwell Ave., in the site previously occupied by Teddy's bar and the Funny Bone comedy club," she wrote. "Shank Hall is the first club venture by owner Peter Jest, whose Alternative Concert Group books shows at the University of Wisconsin–Milwaukee and other venues."

This Shank Hall grand opening flier was posted around town in multiple colors, including neon green and magenta.

Maples noted that "the roster of acts . . . reflects Jest's eclectic book-ing tastes," singling out the contrast between Cervenka, Redbone, New York Voices, and "self-described Jewish-lesbian folk singer" Phranc. Peter had also been booking acts for Bastille Days, a French-themed weekend street festival that took place on the north end of downtown Milwaukee every July. In 1988, he'd booked the Band, which at that time included three of the five original members—Rick Danko, Levon Helm, and Garth Hudson.

On Thursday, the night before it opened to the general public, Shank Hall threw an invite-only party with a cash bar. Peter recorded the take, which was north of a thousand dollars. Friday was the first night the club was open to the public, and a capacity crowd paid four dollars a head to see Java. On Saturday night, the door take was double what it had been the night before, and the bar took in its biggest number yet. Counting Sunday's free show, which also had a cash bar, the club was full on its first four nights.

Peter expected the weekdays to be slower, but as it turned out, capacity was dictated more by the popularity of an act than the day of the week. Reviews of the club itself were generally positive. The rowdy Shank Hall attendees Alderwoman McNamara-McGraw had predicted never materi-alized. Even the local music journalists, who'd seen plenty of venues come and go, were impressed. In his rave review of the New York Voices show, *Milwaukee Journal* jazz critic Mike Drew gave a shout-out to the new venue. "As now set up, the sound system and sight lines are perfect," he wrote.

Running a club and promoting shows in larger venues at the same time meant learning to juggle in a way Peter hadn't before. Though Bob was Peter's 50 percent partner in the business, he wasn't involved in its day-to-day operations. On nights when Peter had something going on at the club and a show he'd promoted somewhere else, he had to choose between the two.

Sometimes it was the club, sometimes it was the show. On Sunday, November 26, 1989, singer-songwriter Syd Straw—who'd been a member of the Golden Palominos and was now touring behind her first solo album, *Surprise*—was playing Shank. Meanwhile, at Green Bay's Riverside Ballroom, the LA-based punk-flavored Red Hot Chili Peppers, who'd been touring all year behind their new release *Mother's Milk*, were performing the fiftieth show of their tour. On Monday, they'd knock off their fifty-first

ALTERNATIVE CONCERT GROUP

& KOSHICK BROS.

—present—

RED HOT CHILI PEPPERS

Sunday, Nov. 26th • 7 p.m. Show

Plus A Special Opening Act To Be Announced

• ALL AGES •

Cash Bar with proper I.D.

RIVERSIDE BALLROOM

115 Newhall (corner Newhall & Main) Green Bay

Tickets available at Riverside Ballroom and all Ticketron/Teletron outlets.

Peter and Jack Koshick teamed up to bring the Red Hot Chili Peppers to Green Bay the weekend after Thanksgiving in 1989.

at Madison's Barrymore Theater. These were the shows Peter had booked with Jack Koshick the previous summer.

Peter opted to skip the Chili Peppers show in Green Bay on Sunday and attend their show in Madison on Monday. The Packers were playing the Vikings in Green Bay Sunday afternoon, but the game would be over well before the Chili Peppers started. He sent a couple of trusted friends, local musicians Mark Shurilla and Rob Czarnezki, to handle the catering, load-in, and load-out for the band.

The Syd Straw show was over when Peter got the call from Rob. "They were naked," he said, "and when the police came after them, they ran."

"What!"

"They're okay," Rob said. "They weren't arrested."

In the age of the twenty-four-hour news cycle, the incident would likely have been all over the media, especially on a slow news day. But it wasn't until about three months later, in February of 1990, that the story made its way to *Spin* magazine, where writer Dean Kuipers described the incident from the band's point of view:

> The Red Hot Chili Peppers stroll quietly into the ballroom and sneak a look around. The crowd is fairly small, strangely restless, buzzing and hurting for relief from the sexual frustrations of a Midwestern farm town winter. Perfect. For the first time on the Mother's Milk tour, the Chilis decide to give them the sock.
>
> Backstage, tour manager Mark Johnson produces a fresh pack of white tube socks. The Chilis rush from the cold dressing room into the friendly, swarming heat of the auditorium wearing tennis shoes, hats and the socks stretched over their cocks—a costume they save these days for stifled places like Green Bay.

What happened next is hardly a surprise—it would have been surprising if the explosive energy onstage *hadn't* resulted in flying footwear and nude musicians. Mark and Rob intercepted the band members as they left the stage to warn them that concert security had called the police, who were on their way.

Rob and Mark were able to get three of the band members—John Frusciante, Chad Smith, and Flea—out, but lead singer Anthony Kiedis

19. **FOOD AND BEVERAGE** - Purchaser to provide twelve (12) hot meals, four (4) of which are to be vegetarian, between soundcheck and showtime. Times and menu to be advised by Artist. Deli trays (enough for twelve (12) people) consisting of assorted meats, cheeses, fruits, vegetables, breads, crackers, chips and dips.

- •Two (2) Cases Corona Beer
- •One (1) bottle Red Wine (Cabernet Sauvignon)
- •Two (2) Bottles Cranberry Juice
- •Two (2) Bottles Grapefruit Juice
- •One (1) Bottle Apple Juice
- •Two (2) Gallons Hot Water
- •Three (3) Gallons Non-Carbonated Spring Water
- •Twenty (20) Large Fresh Clean Towels
- •Two (2) Bars Bath Soap
- •Four (4) Pairs of new White Tube Socks
- •Four (4) Local Sports Team Caps

- •Two (2) Sixpacks Kerns Mango Nectar
- •One (1) Case Coca-Cola Classic
- •One (1) Case Koala Soda
- •One (1) Six-Pack Dr. Pepper
- •Blue Corn Chips & Salsa
- •Large assortment of Chocolates
- •Ice
- •Condiments
- •Bottle openers, Ashtrays and Matches
- •Coffee, Tea, Cream, Sugar, 2 Jars Honey and 5 Fresh Lemons
- •One (1) Carton Winston Cigarettes
- •Plates, Silverware, Cups and Napkins

Purchaser should provide the deli trays and all of the above refreshments in Artist's dressing room approximately one (1) hour prior to showtime.

PLEASE INDICATE YOUR UNDERSTANDING AND ACCEPTANCE OF THE ABOVE BY SIGNING BELOW.

ACCEPTED AND AGREED TO:

BY: _____
PURCHASER

ACCEPTED AND AGREED TO:

BY: _____
ARTIST

4

According to the Red Hot Chili Peppers' tour rider, four fresh pairs of white tube socks were provided to the band before their 1989 Green Bay show. The socks were worn, but not on their feet.

was apprehended by the security team, who held him until the police arrived. The police ended up letting him go. Rob had a friend in the area, so he and Mark spirited the band away to his friend's house and, eventually, reunited them with the rest of their tour team.

Peter was glad to have missed the show. The Peppers would not have liked what he would have said or the volume at which he would have said it. When he did meet the band in Madison the next night, he simply warned them that a repeat of Green Bay's wardrobe choice might not be a good idea. The Chilis, fresh off the excitement and relief of the previous night's close call, chose wisely. The Barrymore show was all music, and the band had no trouble keeping their socks on. They wore them on their feet.

In May of 1990, Peter did his last ever show at the UWM Ballroom, with Robert Fripp and the League of Crafty Guitarists. The aborted UWM Times interview had helped him make the decision to end ACG's existence as a student group. He was enrolled in his usual one-credit class as an auditor that semester, but he knew it should be his last.

A few months earlier, he had struck a deal with Bob Weidenbaum to become the sole owner of Shank Hall. By that time, Peter had eight years of music industry experience. He'd learned enough about the vagaries of the business to have grown accustomed to the tight margins and the constant uncertainty, the adrenaline rush of things going well and how to roll with the punches when they didn't. Bob's career trajectory had been a lot smoother. Graduating college with the grades and LSAT scores to get into and through law school, being admitted to the bar, and earning a steady, dependable living hadn't prepared him for the glacial pace at which a small club moved toward prosperity. As an attorney, Bob was comfortable watching and advising clients as they grew their businesses and careers. But as an investor, he'd hoped for a quicker return.

There was no question for Peter about the right thing to do. The terms of the buyout were generous and realistic. Bob knew Peter was good for the money, and the installments were manageable enough that Peter was able to continue running the club without having to move into his parents' basement with Echo, his six-month-old scarlet macaw. He'd always dreamed of a house filled with pets, asthma be damned. Echo was less time-intensive than a cat or dog and would live a lot longer.

Peter was now the sole owner of a club—and a successful one at that. Shank Hall's first year included shows by former Rolling Stones guitarist Mick Taylor, Doors organist Ray Manzarek, punk poet Jim Carroll, and emerging acts that weren't yet but would become household names, like alt-rockers the Smashing Pumpkins and singer-songwriter Jack Johnson. Shank also hosted the Goo Goo Dolls in April of 1991, several years before they found mainstream success.

Ever since the end of his stint as their tour manager, Peter had been booking Violent Femmes' members Snopek, Balestrieri, DeLorenzo, Gano, and Ritchie at Shank Hall (and sometimes UWM) for gigs as soloists and with other bands. Gano's band, the Mercy Seat, played UWM. One of Balestrieri's bands, the Ghostly Trio (Balestrieri on sax, Tim Taylor on bass, and Geoff Worman on guitar) became a December favorite at Shank for several years. Its take on traditional Christmas songs could best be described as if Brave Combo and Tom Waits had a baby with a punk rocker on quaaludes. Shank was also the venue for a 1991 Femmes show benefiting survivors of a fire that had taken place at the Norman apartment building at 634 West Wisconsin Avenue in downtown Milwaukee, killing four people and leaving many people homeless. The building had been home to a diverse community of local artists who supported one another's lives and work. The show turned out to be drummer Victor DeLorenzo's last gig with the Femmes for many years.

That October, ACG promoted shows in Madison, Milwaukee, and Ames, Iowa, for the triple bill of Pearl Jam, the Smashing Pumpkins, and the Red Hot Chili Peppers, with the Peppers as the headline act and the Smashing Pumpkins as the top supporting band. Reviews of the October 22 show at Milwaukee's Central Park Ballroom don't even mention Pearl Jam, which was touring behind its first album, *Ten*. Those shows—the first three of a national tour—were a big deal for Peter to have scored. He had a history with the agent for the tour, Trip Brown, and it was his word that landed Peter the gig. But that wasn't the only big October event in Peter's life. His friend Randy McElrath, who'd previously owned Stardate Productions, was in the process of opening a Midwest office for Cellar Door Productions, a national company cofounded by Jack Boyle, who, like Peter, started out by owning his own club.

At this 1991 Red Hot Chili Peppers show at the Central Park Ballroom, Pearl Jam opened for special guests Smashing Pumpkins, but the band was so unknown that it wasn't even mentioned on the flyer.

In 1992, when the members of Spinal Tap played their second show in Milwaukee, they held a press conference at Shank Hall before performing at the Riverside Theater.
COURTESY OF RON FAIOLA

Randy reached out to Peter and asked if he'd consider coming to work for him. The job would basically entail doing what Peter was already doing, but with a guaranteed salary and benefits. He just had to consider how working for Cellar Door would affect his ability to book acts for Shank Hall and how, if at all, it would impact ACG.

Peter and Randy set up a formal interview for October 25, 1991. It started out on a somber note, one that had nothing to do with matters at hand. Bill Graham, the pioneering San Francisco–based promoter who, among other things, had put together The Band's *Last Waltz* concert and documentary, had been killed in a helicopter crash in Sonoma County. Peter had seen the news; Randy hadn't. They spent the first part of their

Peter's backstage pass to Spinal Tap's show at the Riverside ostensibly granted him "No Access."

conversation remembering one of the giants of their industry before moving on to the matter of Peter's employment.

When the interview was over, Peter had a new job and a new title: alternative talent buyer. Shank Hall would run as it always had. Alternative Concert Group would go into an extended period of hibernation, lasting as long as he was employed by Cellar Door. Peter would have the opportunity not only to work closely with one of his local heroes, but also to be part of an organization with a national reach. Even if ACG never came out of dormancy, it would be worth it.

8

Rising from the Ashes

The peaceful nowhere of being sound asleep in his comfortable bed was suddenly interrupted. Peter couldn't localize the noise. Struggling to place it amidst the relentlessness of the ringing, which had also roused Echo, he was suddenly awake enough to realize what was happening.

Pulling the bedcovers aside, he noted the time and date—6:30 a.m., September 13, 1992. No need to turn on the light for what was probably a wrong number. He hung up, soothed the bird, and was back to bed and asleep again inside of forty-five seconds. But it started again.

"Hello?"

"Peter?" It was John, who worked at the gas station across from Shank. "Your club is on fire."

The upside was proximity—Peter's apartment on Warren Street was just on the other side of the gas station, a block away from the club. The downside was realizing, as he threw on whatever clothes were closest in his haste to get there, the source of the smoke smell he'd vaguely noticed coming through the open window.

He arrived, winded and reaching for the inhaler he hoped was still in his pocket, as one of the firefighters surrounding Shank's heavy wooden door began swinging an axe to smash through it.

"No!" Peter yelled, breaking through the small crowd of spectators that had gathered to watch the spectacle. "I have a key!"

A firefighter broke from the scrum to put an arm on his shoulder, patting him gently as he guided him back toward the curb. "I'm sorry, son," he said. "It's too late."

Then he turned, lowered the gas mask from the brim of his hat onto his face, and disappeared into the club. Smoke poured from the open door. On the north side of the building, just feet away, firefighters were aiming hoses at the roof. Despite the steady stream of water, smoke and fire continued to rise toward the sky from increasingly expanding holes in the roof until there was nothing left.

Peter watched, first alone, and then with his parents, Tracy, Rob, and other friends and staffers who gradually arrived to stand beside him. TV news cameras filmed the sidewalk scene. Reporters wanted quotes, but there wasn't much to say.

By 9:00 a.m., Peter and his crew were allowed inside. The damage was extensive. They cast their eyes over the twisted metal and melted glass poking up from a thick sea of wet ash. The air was pure campfire, heavy with particulates. Overhead, the sun streamed in from the bare expanse that had once been a closed roof, now open to the sky.

Peter waded through the mess, water soaking through his shoes and debris clinging to the bottom of his pants until he reached his office. The safe was wet, but intact. His landlord, Jim Wiechmann, joined him in a walk through the club. From the midpoint between the stage and Peter's office, Jim turned a slow circle, surveying the extent of the damage. The fire department had brought him down to confirm that Peter was up to date on rent. (He was.) They also wanted to know whether Peter and Wiechmann had insurance. (They did.) The department was doing its due diligence, starting the investigation at the earliest stage possible. Ruling out arson was a necessary step.

The bottled beer in the cooler room close to the bar was intact. Still, even though it was perfectly drinkable, who knew when—or if—he'd ever serve another customer.

Peter walked to the space where the door had been. "Hey!" he called to anyone within listening distance. From around the room, his team turned—six pairs of eyes on him, expectant, waiting to hear what he could possibly say as they stood in what was left of their workplace. "Let's divide up the beer and everyone can take some home," he said.

"I could use one now," said Rob.

"Good idea." Peter walked back to the cooler, fished out bottles, and handed them out as someone else checked to see if the opener attached to the bar was still operational.

They were standing together on the sidewalk in front of the club, drinking, when a man with a camera walked up, trailed by two more with notebooks. Peter recognized Bill Meyer, the *Sentinel* photographer, who'd been shooting the fire. Peter had already talked to the paper's reporters.

"Can I get a photo?" Bill asked. Peter followed him inside to a spot of his choosing, one that included a good view of what was left of the club's sound equipment setup. It wasn't until Peter saw the paper the next day that he realized he hadn't put down the bottle of Heineken. It wasn't a big deal, it was just that under normal circumstances, he wouldn't have posed for a photo with a beer—and he also didn't drink alcohol at that hour of the day.

At noon, his ride pulled up. Peter had to turn things at Shank Hall over to Rob and go to Madison for his Cellar Door job. U2 was playing Camp

The *Milwaukee Sentinel* captioned this photo: "Peter Jest, owner of Shank Hall, 1434 N. Farwell Ave., looks over the charred remains of the club Sunday after an early morning fire." An accompanying headline read, "Owner Considers Closing Down."
© MILWAUKEE JOURNAL SENTINEL - USA TODAY NETWORK

Randall Stadium that night, and it was an all-hands-on-deck situation. Bev, a friend who owned Milwaukee's Toad Café, was going to the show, and she and Peter had already planned to ride together. The show had sold out months earlier, and the 62,000 ticket holders did not care about a club fire in Milwaukee.

"I'll try to call later," he told Rob.

Bev took her cue from Peter, who was silent for most of the ride, wondering what was happening back in Milwaukee and trying to focus on what he'd be doing in Madison. No one died or got hurt, he told himself. That was what really mattered. And Rob could handle any media outlets that showed up wanting an interview.

Bev dropped him at the stadium gate, where he entered what was basically a pop-up small town. The advance crew had been at Camp Randall for five days, setting up the stage, lights, and sound equipment. As Peter walked past the rows of semis and turned onto one of the makeshift avenues running between the trailers serving as dressing rooms and offices, he noticed the smell of ash, an odd contrast to the clear blue sky overhead. In the time it took for Peter to find Cellar Door's trailer, he'd figured out the source of the odor: him. Catching his reflection in a window, he realized that, with his rumpled clothes and mussed hair, he looked like Pigpen from Charlie Brown. At the best of times, Peter looked just short of disheveled. Today, he'd gone past that and then some. It occurred to him—too late—that maybe he should have asked Bev to swing by his apartment for a change of clothes.

When his boss, Randy, saw him, he reached for his wallet. "You smell like an ashtray," he said, handing Peter a wad of bills, then pulling a hotel key from his pocket. "I'm in Room 341. Buy yourself a change of clothes and come back after you take a shower."

Peter's place in the Cellar Door food chain worked in his favor that day. He typically handled all the heavy lifting for smaller shows and anything in a theater. It was Randy's job to do the same for arena and stadium shows. Everyone pitched in, but Peter's main function at the U2 concert was to be available. On bigger productions like this one, he handled the marketing component. That meant writing and disseminating press releases, placing ads in various media outlets, and ensuring that all expenses were properly recorded and receipts for those expenses were on hand at the venue in case anyone associated with the band wanted to see them. The paper trail mattered, because for the U2 show, the band was guaranteed a set amount if a certain number of tickets were sold (say, ten thousand). For any tickets sold above that number, the band got a percentage of the sales after expenses, including marketing. The band's management had a right to verify what the promoter was claiming as expenses, and because Peter was the marketing point person, he was the one who would be called on to answer any questions.

When the concert began, he and Randy watched from the back of the stadium. Peter recognized that it was a great show, but he couldn't keep his mind off the mess he knew he had to go back to the next day.

The front page of Monday's *Milwaukee Journal* featured a shot of U2 lead singer Bono onstage at Camp Randall, with a teaser to a full story and review on page 5 of the Metro section. The top story on the Metro section's front page read, "Fire Damages Shank Hall." According to the article, the fire had caused an estimated $100,000 worth of damage. Firefighters speculated that a lit cigarette accidentally dropped on a couch backstage had caused the blaze; the fire department ultimately confirmed that this was the case.

Once he made it home and had some time to rest, Peter was ready to take on the big questions about what to do. He walked over to the club—where he'd changed up the marquee from the usual upcoming band name to "We're Toast!"—and noticed some additional, less formal signage on the front wall. Someone had chalked "Ha ha he he ho ho!!!" just to the right of the front door. That a random heckler was reveling in his possible demise was an aha moment for Peter. That was the moment he knew for sure he had to reopen.

In the meantime, though, he had artists booked to play in what was now a burnt shell. Plenty of shows would end up being canceled, but not all. Peter pivoted to his preclub days as a promoter needing to find a venue. Because Milwaukee was a small enough community and Peter's day job at Cellar Door meant regular contact with venues in Milwaukee and beyond, he was well positioned to salvage some dates. He tried to move as many shows as he could to wherever he could—rescheduling some at smaller local venues like the City Club, Celebrity Club, and the Unicorn.

Before taking off for the U2 show in Madison, Peter had spoken briefly with his lawyer, Bob Weidenbaum, and his landlord, Jim Wiechmann, about the insurance situation. Bob had appeared the next morning with a camera. "We're going to photograph everything," he told Peter, explaining that the insurance company was going to want confirmation of every asset they listed on the claim form. He wasn't kidding. Everything meant everything, including the snow shovel he had Peter hold at arm's length for a photo, capturing enough of the background to indicate that it was club property.

That attention to detail paid off. The insurance settlements Peter and Jim received from their respective companies enabled them, very literally, to build back better. Peter kept the fixtures pretty much the same as they had been—cocktail tables and comfortable-but-functional chairs. But he hired skilled professionals for the construction work, and he and Jim collaborated on upgrades. Jim would let him know when there was a choice to be made, then direct the contractor to carry out the work according to Peter's preferences. Among the changes was the addition of one exit door and a women's toilet and sink, which increased the club's capacity from 240 to 300.

A little over three months after the fire, Shank Hall 2.0 was ready. The club reopened December 18, with Minneapolis-based rock band Trip Shakespeare as the headline act. In an advance story that ran in the *Milwaukee Journal*, Peter joked that the first one hundred people to arrive at the show would receive books of "Shank Hall commemorative matches." Once again, Peter's day job with Cellar Door meant relying on Rob, Tracy, and the rest of his crew to make sure everything was in order at Shank Hall— and also relying on the neighbor who looked in on Echo when Peter was away. Two days before the reopening, Peter, Randy, and the rest of the Cellar Door crew had flown down to Fort Lauderdale, where the company was headquartered, for its annual Christmas party. Back in Milwaukee, Peter's staff was scrambling to get things prepared for the moment doors opened. A driver delivering beer that afternoon walked in, took one look at the workers installing the last of the ceiling tiles, and told Sue, who managed the bar, that there was no way Shank would be opening that night. He was wrong. The club was at capacity when Trip Shakespeare took the stage, the best possible conclusion to a potentially career-ending incident.

In the months after the fire, Peter felt fortunate to have his job at Cellar Door—even if it was turning out to be less of a good fit than he'd anticipated. He liked working with Randy, the regular paycheck, paid vacation, health insurance, and the camaraderie of coworkers he didn't have to supervise. But the business model that had existed when Peter got his first job in the industry in 1982 was in the process of being replaced by a centralized, top-down structure, and now he was watching it happen from the inside. The era of a Steve Mandelman mentoring a teenage Peter Jest in exchange for cheap labor was disappearing. Companies like Cellar Door wanted to work with established international acts—Elton John, U2 —and those clearly on their way to that level, and that's where Cellar Door and its competitors were putting their focus. In-house experts tracking metrics like record and ticket sales were driving booking decisions at all levels, not the gut feelings of low-level staffers in Flyover Country.

These changes in the industry were affecting the entire ecosystem. Agents needed to go where the money was, and when an artist hit a certain level, the money was with the Cellar Doors of the world. Peter's presence at Cellar Door was a value-add because of his relationships. He enabled the company to do shows with Arlo Guthrie, John Prine, and other midlevel draws. He was still operating on the principle that if you built a relationship with an act while it was drawing an audience of fifty to two hundred, the act would stick with you later, when it was drawing thousands. But Peter was bumping up against an uncomfortable realization—that developing relationships with emerging artists was less of a priority for the company than it was for him.

In 1992, Peter, in his role at Cellar Door, had booked two dates with an up-and-coming artist that he felt certain was going to become a big-name act: Sarah McLachlan. He'd negotiated to bring her to Club de Wash in Madison for $500 and to Shank Hall in Milwaukee for $1,000. Randy's reaction to the booking had been lukewarm, a variation on "Is this really the kind of thing we want to be doing?" The shows were small potatoes to Cellar Door, but believing in emerging acts like McLachlan was exactly what Peter found exciting about his job. At that moment, a nagging feeling began to set in that his days at Cellar Door would soon be over.

In the meantime, he continued to benefit from the job. For one thing, he had the direct experience of working closely for a boss who could remain calm when things were about to fall apart. Watching Randy in a crisis was instructive, and it would inform the way Peter worked going forward. The job also helped him make the transition from tenant to homeowner. In April of 1993, he bought a house on Milwaukee's East Side. As a salaried employee, he was able to navigate the mortgage application process without raising any of the questions a bank might have had for a self-employed independent promoter. The house had the two things Peter was really looking for: a north-facing sunroom with a bank of windows that would serve as a bird room for Echo and a fenced-in back yard for an eventual dog. The house was also big enough to be comfortable for two people. Earlier in the year, a conversation with a cute, dark-haired woman who'd come to the club had grown into something bigger. He and Cynthia Stanford turned out to have a lot in common. They were both Milwaukee natives around thirty years old and both entrepreneurs—she had her own catering business. Peter had asked her out, and they'd gotten engaged in March.

After setting up his office, Echo's bird room, and a place to sleep, Peter turned his attention to furnishing the rest of the place. In addition to a new desk and file cabinet, he brought a bed, dresser (the same one he'd been using since childhood), chair, and TV from his apartment on Warren Street. He splurged on a new sofa and raided his parents' basement for a kitchen table and chairs.

By August, though, Peter was single again. He had known it wasn't going to work when Cynthia asked him to stop seeing his female friends without her after they were married, regardless of the circumstances. After the breakup, he went back to his regular pattern of serial dating, but, when he had the time to think about it, he hoped for a more consistent type of companionship.

The Friday before Labor Day weekend, he and his friend Leslie LaForce took a drive to the Elmbrook Humane Society. Strolling along the cage-lined hallway, they paused periodically to inspect a particular dog and read its story. When they got to a five-year-old male German shepherd/ Sheltie mix, Peter stopped, remembering a dog his family had occasionally watched during his childhood when its owners were out of town. He and the animal surveyed each other, the dog stretched out on the floor of its cage as Peter knelt, silent and still, watching the dog watch him. Zach had been surrendered by his former owners. There was no information about why. Peter didn't care. On the way home, they hit the pet store for a collar, leash, bed, toys, food, and treats.

Peter and his scarlet macaw, Echo, in the backyard of their East Side house.

In addition to being the fulfillment of a promise Peter had made to his younger self, Zach helped Peter reestablish a routine. Work hours began after a morning walk. Zach would relax or nap under Peter's desk while he made calls and managed paperwork. In the afternoon, they took another walk, after which Peter would wind up the office portion of his workday.

As often as not, walks would turn into informal social outings. Neighbors who'd seen Echo through the window would pet the dog, then ask Peter about the bird. Zach turned out to be well trained and friendly— at least, with anyone who wasn't a postal carrier or UPS driver. Peter took Zach to his parents', his sister's, parties—pretty much everywhere except his brother's house (Tim was too allergic) and the club. When Peter had to

Alanis
Morissette

Alanis Morissette played Shank Hall on July 25, 1995—about a month after the release of her album *Jagged Little Pill* and five months before she was on the cover of *Rolling Stone* thanks to her breakout hit, "You Oughta Know." Peter knew, which is why he jumped at the chance to have her play Shank Hall for five hundred dollars.

attend a show out of town, Marvin and Kathryn would take Zach to their house. If Peter knew he was going to have a late night, a neighbor would come over to walk the dog.

Zach was a bright spot in a tough year for Peter's love life and a tumultuous one in terms of his work. In October, Cellar Door's main office directed Randy to tell Peter that he could continue working there only if he accepted a different pay arrangement. It basically amounted to a straight commission with benefits. Peter had two weeks to decide, but the decision wasn't a hard one. Walking away from the job was relatively easy, especially because it wasn't a bitter separation.

With his home office set up, Peter began working on bringing Alternative Concert Group out of dormancy. Randy had given him a head start, letting Peter promote the remaining shows he'd booked while at Cellar Door as ACG instead, including the Violent Femmes in November at the Barrymore in Madison and New Age pianist David Lanz that same month at the Riverside in Milwaukee.

Shank Hall highlights from 1993 included an April 28 show featuring Widespread Panic, touring behind their newest album, *Everyday*, and a December 8 solo show with Steve Howe, the guitarist of the English progressive rock band Yes. In between were dates with Bela Fleck and the Flecktones, Iris Dement, and the Gufs. Overhearing Howe's first impression of Shank made a lasting impression on Peter, who was by the door when Howe and his tour manager walked in. "See?" Howe told his manager. "A bar doesn't have to smell like stale beer." Later, Howe let Peter know he was impressed that the club had provided everything he'd asked for in his rider.

About a month later, in the first days of 1994, the Violent Femmes hosted a benefit for WMSE at Shank Hall. The nonprofit radio station housed at the Milwaukee School of Engineering boasted an all-volunteer on-air staff with presenters who were experts in their particular genre. A point of pride for the station was broadcasting music and information not available on mainstream outlets. In addition to raising money for the station, the Femmes' Shank show was the first featuring drummer Guy Hoffman, who had replaced Victor DeLorenzo. It was the type of show that made Peter feel good about his work—providing a stage to raise money in the name of independent music. On the opposite end of the spectrum, a show in April was a lesson in the type of shows he wanted to avoid.

A year to the day after the 1993 Widespread Panic show at Shank, Peter was pacing the lobby of the Barrymore Theater waiting for Rickie Lee Jones. The rain that had been falling since morning wasn't letting up, increasing the anticipation at the same time that it was dampening—in the most literal way—the excitement of the audience for Jones's nearly sold-out show. Peter had been in high school the first time he saw her in 1978; his parents had driven him to and from that show. Tonight, they were watching Zach. Jones was late, and Peter was pretty sure he knew why. Performers who think they can make it from Chicago to Madison in an hour and a half are not accounting for the traffic that almost always surrounds Chicago.

This wasn't a Leo Kottke situation where someone qualified could step in for sound check. Before Jones arrived, Peter made a request of her production manager, who was already there: would he mind if they allowed ticket holders, who were currently lined up around the block, into the lobby? "These are her fans," Peter said. "Can we at least get them out of the rain?"

"Sure," the production manager answered. "Let's get 'em in the lobby."

Since it was Peter's first time working with Jones, and he had heard she could be difficult, he called and ran the plan by Jones's manager in Los Angeles, just to cover his bases. The manager also said, "Sure, go for it. That'll be fine."

When Jones finally arrived and began her sound check, she was immediately distracted by the sound of people talking inside the lobby. "What are those people doing here?" she demanded. "Who let those people in here? Where's the promoter?"

When Peter identified himself, Jones dressed him down from the stage. "There might not be any show tonight!" she threatened, before slamming down her guitar and walking into the dressing room. Peter was, frankly, pissed. Not only did he feel demeaned in front of his coworkers, his crew, and the Barrymore's crew, but he had also tried to do everything right. If Jones had simply gone to her tour manager to complain, he could have explained everything to her. Instead, she'd done it in front of everybody— even her fans in the lobby had heard the yelling.

When Jones went on, she played three songs before acknowledging the audience. She said nothing about the scene that had preceded the show, deciding instead to apologize to Peter at the end of the night. Peter was annoyed. She should have apologized on stage. He never worked with Jones again, despite being offered a chance to do so. His career was solid enough that he could afford the luxury of not working with performers whose professionalism began and ended on stage.

Later that year, on August 14, 1994, Peter was turning thirty. His singular focus since walking into Steve Mandelman's house twelve years earlier had been on building a career. Now, he was in a position to look back at where he'd been and be more strategic about life going forward. He had a house and a little family of his own with Zach and Echo. He had time to watch sports and his favorite old TV sitcoms. What else was there? The answer, in part, turned out to be motorcycles and muskies.

In the spring of 1994, Peter had taken a motorcycle class with his friends Tammy and Kathy. Their husbands—Bob Babisch, his former boss at Summerfest, and Bob Weidenbaum, his lawyer—were friends with Peter and with each other. Both men owned Harley-Davidson motorcycles, and Tammy and Kathy had decided to get their licenses, too. When the class was over, Peter bought a used Honda, which he rode for one season before trading up to a Harley.

Earlier that year, he had gone to the Milwaukee Sentinel Sports Show with an eye toward finding a dog-friendly resort in the North Woods where he could do some fishing. He'd chosen Evergreen Lodge in Boulder Junction in Vilas County, roughly six hours north of Milwaukee. The lodge, open since 1929, was on Little Crooked Lake. He'd never been to the lodge, but Boulder Junction was part of his childhood. His mother's brother Jack, who'd died when Peter was young, had lived there, and Peter remembered visiting.

During his first few trips to the lodge, Peter was constantly on the phone, checking his answering machine, and booking shows. After a while, the lodge owners felt so sorry for him that they set him up with a fishing guide. Eventually, Peter got the hang of the work/fishing balance. The second year he and Zach spent time there, he hired Jeff, a guide who lived next door to the lodge with his wife and small children. Over the decades, what started out as business transactions—between Peter and Evergreen's owners, Noel and Laurel, and between Peter and Jeff—deepened into friendships. When Jeff's daughter Rachel moved to Milwaukee in 1993, Peter hired her to work at Shank Hall. Rachel began dating Ed, who worked the door. Eventually, they married and moved back to Boulder Junction, where Ed ended up working as a fishing guide. Laurel would meet Peter in Wausau or Stevens Point, at his invitation, whenever he had a show there.

There was a lot about going up north that kept Peter coming back. His fishing family never cared about what Peter did for a living. It was one of the rare spaces—physical and metaphysical—where he was able to

Peter at Evergreen Lodge in 1998. By then, he'd gotten the hang of balancing work and vacation time and had become an adequate fisherman.

consciously put the music business out of his mind and focus on a different kind of challenge. Those worlds came together when Rachel and Ed met and married. But the focus always was, and remained, on the friendships. And, of course, the fish.

9

Fine Milwaukee Water

One night in 1997, in the hours leading up to a Leo Kottke show at Madison's Barrymore Theater, Peter found himself in trouble. The problem was a small upright piano. "[It] was missing a string and the keys were uneven," Kottke remembered years later. "I mean, this thing was just wretched. It wasn't a piano anymore. . . . It was out of tune, and to tune it would be dangerous." Kottke didn't play the piano, but on this particular night, he was performing with Iris Dement, and she did. So, he started badgering Peter for a better piano.

Something similar had once happened to Kottke at a show on the East Coast with a different promoter. He had been playing at a new venue and discovered during sound check that its sound system had a terrible board. Sound systems—which typically include amps, monitors, microphones, and speakers—are controlled through a sound or mixing board. Before an audience arrives at a show, performers do their sound checks with the audio engineer. Some acts travel with their own sound systems, but most rely on an in-house person and venue-owned or promoter-rented equipment.

Sound checks are done to ensure perfect or near-perfect alignment between what the artist wants the audience to hear from the stage and what the audience actually hears. And Leo Kottke was fastidious about his sound checks. Most artists make somewhat general requests of an engineer—to turn down the midrange, maybe, or increase the high or low end—and then they repeat the process until they get the results they're after. Kottke, on the other hand, would call out his instructions in decibel ranges. He'd walk into a hall with his guitar in hand, sit in an empty seat, and play from there in order to hear exactly how the notes he was playing would be heard by the people filling the seats hours later. So, it was no small thing for him to encounter a substandard board. The promoter said he'd procure a replacement, then didn't. By the time Kottke realized what had happened, there was nothing to be done but perform the show as best he could.

Kottke credited his booking agent for the fact that incidents like that one happened to him so rarely. "This was the second time in fifty years," he said, "and this has happened mainly because I go through a good booking agent. If you've got a good agent, you're lucky, because they know who to work with, and mine works with Peter."

Peter could have asked Kottke and Iris Dement to use the subpar piano at the Barrymore. "Iris wasn't pushing for it," Kottke remembered. "She said, 'I don't care, this will be all right.'" But he was pushing. And Peter responded. One of the stagehands knew where to get a rental electric piano keyboard on short notice, and Peter was able to make that happen.

His first time booking Leo Kottke, at UWM in April of 1984, was an experience he would never forget. As it turned out, Leo remembered it, too. "I remember getting lost and having to call him," he recalled, "and I remember that part of the problem was finding a phone. . . . I got there on time, but I'm sure I scared him to death." One thing Peter didn't know then was that he wasn't the first, and wouldn't be the last, promoter to have that particular Leo Kottke experience. "I've done it with other promoters too," he admitted, "so Peter wasn't the only one."

Peter and Leo's second show—in March of 1986, also at UWM—was much less eventful. There was no missed turnoff, no hunting for phones, no need for apologies. Just an appreciative audience, an evening of great music, and, after he and Peter had conducted their postshow business, two words. Two words that Leo never failed to utter at the conclusion of one of the shows he did with Peter—which would turn out to be somewhere between seventy and eighty shows and counting. Those two words would distinguish Leo from hundreds of other acts Peter promoted. Unlike many other acts, Leo was his own tour manager and personally settled accounts with Peter at the end of the night. It always stood out to Peter that Leo never left a venue without saying thank you.

Leo felt equally positive about Peter, with one very loud exception: Echo, Peter's scarlet macaw. As a musician and a man whose hearing was

Leo Kottke and Peter backstage after Leo's show at Oshkosh's Grand Opera House in 1997.

damaged during his service in the US Navy, Leo was understandably very protective of his hearing. And anyone who had ever been on a call with Peter from his home office and heard Echo through the receiver could sympathize with Leo's position. At any moment, a conversation could be abruptly interrupted, or sometimes accompanied, by a live performance of otherworldly screeches and squawks. "When I think of Peter," Leo ruminated in 2022, "I always think of the noise where he lives, that goddamn bird he lives with. When [birds like that] go off, it's like a grenade, an amplitude of 130 decibels. They're like the muzzle of a twelve-gauge."

Echo aside, Leo and Peter established a genuine connection over their decades working together. "There's kind of a congenial aspect I've always looked forward to seeing," Leo said about working with Peter. "Usually you don't see the promoter at these jobs, and if you do, it's brief."

It was 1998 when Peter first booked Leo together with Leon Redbone. It was a three-show, three-city tour—the Barrymore in Madison, the Grand in Oshkosh, and the Pabst in Milwaukee. But the two musicians had been friends and touring mates long before Peter thought to put them on the same bill; when they first met, Peter was probably in grade school. "We went to Germany twice and Australia twice," Leo remembered of his early touring days with Leon, "the first time as support and the second time as a double bill."

Back in 1986, when Peter had first booked Redbone at Century Hall, the agent Elizabeth Rush had warned him to leave the musician alone. Peter had no problem doing that, and the show had gone off without a hitch. The next few dates they did together followed the pattern of the first. Then—slowly, but surely—Leon began engaging. He started asking Peter questions and talking about old music. Over the course of those interactions, they discovered they had a similar sense of humor and got along well.

Leon also found out firsthand how Peter operated when something went wrong. On the third Saturday of Shank Hall's existence as a club, Leon had been scheduled to play two shows. Peter—who had booked an ACG show at UWM with jazz violinist Jean Luc Ponty for that same night—couldn't be at the club. Leon's first show was uneventful. But between sets, the sound engineer, who'd been sent by the company Peter hired, wandered into the back of the newly opened club to take a nap. He didn't tell anyone, and when it was time for the second show, no one could find him. Peter's staff looked everywhere they thought he might be, made an announcement, and looked some more. They called Peter and explained the situation. Leon wanted to go on, but performing the show without a sound engineer wasn't an option. The second show was canceled; Peter paid Leon in full and refunded every ticket buyer. As Shank's staff was cleaning up, the engineer wandered out from where he'd been sleeping, ready to work.

Incidents like that one were probably part of the reason Tom Roberts, who played piano on several Leon tours, remembered Shank Hall as a place they looked forward to playing—and remembered Peter as being very different from many of the promoters they encountered. Peter, Tom recalled, was "not lost in what the illusion of a promoter should be. He was very professional and very courteous, and comparing him to the other owners of clubs that I experienced during that time, there was none of that, like, slimy hipster thing."

Redbone also was one of a very few artists to see Peter's house. In addition to a shared sense of humor, they were both animal lovers. At his home in New Hope, Pennsylvania, Leon and his wife, Beryl, had dogs and cats.

Beryl Handler (left), Leon Redbone's wife and manager, with Peter and Leon (right) at the Barrymore Theater in 2007.

By the early 2000s, Peter's nonhuman family included Echo the scarlet macaw, Zach the dog, and Oliver the cat, who ended up being the subject of a series of photos taken by Leon. Leon's visit to Chez Jest was a one-off, but when Leon had a day off between shows, they'd sometimes spend time together over breakfast or lunch.

Wisconsin audiences loved the 1998 Kottke/Redbone shows enough that Peter played the two around the state again in 1999, 2001, 2007, and 2010. Peter got a kick out of watching them interact. For the most part, Leon made jokes and Leo laughed at him. Out of Leon's classic shticks, one of Peter's favorites involved the endless search for a chair, which Peter had experienced the first time he booked Leon. Guitarists like armless chairs, for obvious reasons: chair arms and guitar necks don't mix well. The right chair is crucial for a musician's ability to sit in a position that maximizes their particular musculature. Leon would wander through a venue, auditioning every armless chair he encountered. Peter would follow behind, watching as he homed in on a particular target, then serving as a one-man audience for Leon's latest performance of "Is This the Right Chair?" He'd sit, wiggle around some, then get up and try another. And another. After testing every chair in the building, he'd finally settle on one.

Leo Kottke and Leon Redbone performed together at venues around Wisconsin, including Madison's Barrymore Theater.

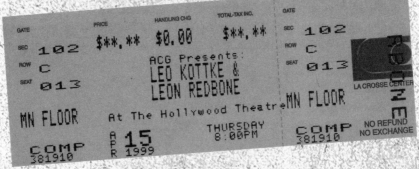

GATE SEC 102 ROW C SEAT 013

PRICE $**.** HANDLING CHG $0.00 TOTAL-TAX INC. $**.**

GATE SEC 102 ROW C SEAT 013

ACG Presents: LEO KOTTKE & LEON REDBONE

MN FLOOR At The Hollywood Theatre MN FLOOR

THURSDAY 8:00PM

COMP 381910 APR 15 1999

COMP 381910

LA CROSSE CENTER

NO REFUND NO EXCHANGE

Who won the toss for this show on the 1999 series of dates is lost to history, but having Peter flip a coin to see who would open the shows Leon and Leo played together was serious business. **PHOTO BY ELLY GRISWOLD**

ACG PRESENTS

Two Sold Out Shows in Wisconsin

Legendary Singer, Songwriter

JOHN PRINE

with
very special guest

LEON REDBONE!

Friday, March 26, 2004
Madison Civic Center

&

Saturday, March 27, 2004
Riverside Theatre • Milwaukee

Leon Redbone occasionally opened for John Prine on tours in Wisconsin.

He was also known for having a glass of Jagermeister on stage with him while he played. Peter remembers audience members shouting, on more than one occasion: "Leon! What are you drinking?"

"Fine Milwaukee water!" he would respond. "It's quite delicious! But you must do something about your pipes!" Leon was never out of character. The person concertgoers saw on stage was the person he was in real life.

Every Kottke/Redbone show started backstage in a similar standoff: no one wanted the headliner slot. Leon didn't want to go on after Leo. Leo, for his part, hated following Leon. Peter recalled Leo telling him, "Leon just takes all the air out of the room because he's so funny." Peter turned it into a game when he started wearing a referee's shirt to their shows. Between sound check and doors, he'd referee the coin toss that determined who went on first.

One night at the Sentry Theater in Stevens Point, Leo lost the toss and had to play after Leon. Later that night, when Leo was on stage, he started telling the crowd a story between songs. All of a sudden, laughter erupted. But Leo hadn't been saying anything he'd intended to be funny. After his initial bewilderment, he realized the audience was looking past him and turned around to see what had captured the room's attention. Poking out from the curtain was a twirling hat on one end of a cane; Leon was behind the curtain, working the other end.

"He could be deadly," Kottke said of Redbone. "He was a phenomenon. I've never laughed harder with anyone on or off stage than Leon. It was right out of Vaudeville, and god, it was beyond funny. It was so quaint. You don't expect quaint to take you anywhere, but you could take it anywhere with Leon."

10

Practically a Guthrie

Way back in 1977, Arlo Guthrie had been touring behind his album *Amigo* when twelve-year-old Peter won a pair of tickets to see him at Summerfest in Milwaukee. He already knew who Arlo was. Peter Meyer, a neighbor across the alley who was close in age to Peter's older brothers, was an Arlo fan. The Meyers and Jests were close—the families socialized together in addition to being neighbors. Older Peter spent a lot of time in the rocking chair in his family's living room, listening to Arlo's catchy melodies and conversational singing style through a pair of then-state-of-the-art headphones. When younger Peter wanted to know what all the fuss was about, older Peter put the headphones over his ears. Younger Peter was hooked. Winning a pair of tickets to see Arlo play the first of two shows at Summerfest with Pete Seeger was a big deal. It was one of the first live shows Peter attended, and one of his first times seeing an artist whose work he already knew.

In 1978, Peter won tickets to see Arlo perform with his band Shenandoah at the Performing Arts Center in July. His rating for the show was a 3 out of 4.

Seven years later, Peter was able to book Arlo himself, bringing him to the Wisconsin Room at UWM. Instead of the calm disposition he usually had when interacting with artists he booked, Peter was nervous. He had become familiar with Leo Kottke's music because he was promoting him. He had watched Leon Redbone's *Saturday Night Live* appearances on the TV in his family's den as a high school student. But Arlo had been a presence in Peter's life long before his tour bus pulled up to the loading dock at the union on the afternoon of October 20.

Of course, to Arlo, Peter was just another promoter with whom his booking agent had negotiated a date. But the date went well enough that they did it again in 1987. Peter brought him to Madison's Barrymore Theater in 1988 and the Riverside Ballroom in Green Bay the following year. Shortly after two more Wisconsin Arlo shows were announced in 1990, Peter got a phone call from a stranger who identified himself as Mark Nerenhausen. "I'm the new executive director at Oshkosh's Grand Opera House," he said, "and I see you're bringing Arlo Guthrie to Madison. I think he'd play very well in Oshkosh."

In the days following that conversation, Peter began researching other small markets in Wisconsin and discovering, in the process, beautiful old working theaters and other concert venues around the state. When Arlo's booking agent called to let Peter know what dates Arlo had available in 1991, ACG made offers for four. Arlo ended up playing shows in Milwaukee's Avalon Theater, the Barrymore in Madison, Oshkosh's Grand Opera House, and the Sentry Theater at the University of Wisconsin–Stevens Point.

Nerenhausen had been right. The September 21, 1991, show at the opera house was a sellout. Three decades later, Nerenhausen can still conjure up that night in his mind. "I remember [Arlo] playing 'Can't Help Falling in Love with You' and the audience singing along," he said. "Of course, his comments about Pete Seeger were also a great part of the show, . . . hearing that firsthand connection with a music legend like that. It says a lot that after presenting hundreds of shows in venues around the country, the magic of that evening sticks with me."

In 1994, Peter booked Arlo at Shank Hall, the Grand Theater in Wausau, the Capitol Civic Centre in Manitowoc, the Viterbo College of Fine Arts in La Crosse, the Grand Opera House in Oshkosh, and the Schofield Auditorium in Eau Claire. Over the course of thirty-eight years, Peter probably booked about a hundred shows with Arlo. In that time, he brought the musician to venues including the Meyer Theater in Green Bay; the Peterson Auditorium in Ishpeming, Michigan; the Hollywood Theater in La Crosse; the South Milwaukee Performing Arts Center and Pabst Theater in Milwaukee; and the State Theatre in Eau Claire.

It might have been Peter's habit of staying out of the way. It might have been that he wasn't much older than Arlo's son, Abe. There's no question

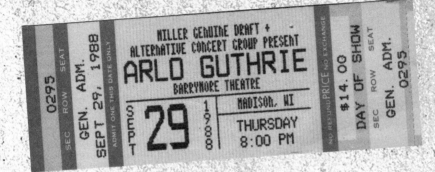

Ten days before bringing the Red Hot Chili Peppers to Green Bay's Riverside Ballroom, Peter and Jack Koshick brought Arlo Guthrie to the same venue.

ACG & KOSHICK BROS.
ALTERNATIVE CONCERT GROUP

—present—

A Solo Evening With
ARLO GUTHRIE

Thursday,
Nov. 16th
8:00 p.m.
showtime

...only area
appearance!

RIVERSIDE BALLROOM
115 Newhall (corner Newhall & Main) Green Bay

Tickets available at Riverside Ballroom and all
Ticketron/Teletron outlets.
$12.50 Advance $15.00 At the Door

This pass dates back to 2006, when Arlo toured celebrating his fortieth anniversary as a touring musician.

that it was, at least partly, the success of the shows. Whatever it was, the alchemy that transforms a neutral or pleasant interaction between relative strangers into a relationship built on mutual trust and respect took place between Peter and Arlo relatively early. As Arlo recalled,

> After the first few dates, we didn't have a contract. We didn't need one. His word was good. And we would show up as planned.
> I didn't feel like I was just a client. I felt like I could help him expand into these other areas because we were riding pretty high at that time, throughout the late eighties and into the nineties. So, it was a mutually beneficial arrangement. And I felt very, very comfortable. Not just with the shows and the promotion, but with everything. I mean the catering. I mean the things you wouldn't think of, but those are the things that make you want to go back. It's not the venues themselves. It's not the people who staff their venues, although most of the time they're really nice. But it's who you know and how you feel about who you know. And it was nice to work with Peter. I never heard a complaint [or] a grumble or [saw] a sour face. There was always somebody who was welcoming and happy to see us. And we were always happy to be there.

Everything logistics-related was arranged between Peter and Arlo's booking agent, which is still standard operating procedure for touring artists. A promoter tenders an offer for a show date and terms, such as one or two performances on a certain date or multiple consecutive dates either at the same venue or in multiple cities. The agent forwards the offer to the artist's manager, who may or may not share it with the artist. Some artists want input on those decisions; others empower their managers to make the calls. Arlo was an input guy.

Agents always want to put the most advantageous offers in front of an artist's manager. But what constitutes "advantageous" can get squishy and depends on multiple factors. The money isn't always the most important thing, although it certainly isn't insignificant. Other factors could include an artist's travel preferences (including the distance between venues), their feelings about a particular venue, and whether they had a bad experience somewhere or heard from someone they trust who did.

Not every promoter is a good fit for every artist, and vice versa. Any given work setting has a particular culture, and different people fit better in some environments than others. Putting on a concert involves a lot of moving parts, a lot of personalities, and a slew of unknowns. It's like any relationship—sometimes the first date goes well and you stick with it. Sometimes one date is enough to know you don't want a second one.

Arlo and Peter's relationship was a best-case scenario. For their earliest shows together, Arlo relied exclusively on the wisdom of his booking agents. But after he'd worked with Peter a few times, Arlo shut down his then-agent (and, later, his two successors) when they recommended that he go with what they considered to be better offers. "We don't have to work with him," Arlo recalled the agents saying, and in response, he said, "No. We work with that guy. That's who, in that territory. That belongs to Peter Jest. We work with Peter Jest."

A significant reason for Arlo's loyalty was Peter's grasp of the big picture. The average concertgoer sees an announcement, buys a ticket, shows up, enjoys themselves for an evening, and goes home. They don't think about everything that's happened to make that experience possible. "Most people," Arlo said in 2022, "don't understand the details of what it takes to put on a show. I mean, I retired a year and a half ago. And it's not so much the gigs. It was the getting there that I retired from. The gigs were easy. Once you walk out on stage and there's an audience there, you got all the energy you need."

For decades, Arlo's road manager would make sure everyone got where they needed to be with enough lead time to set up the stage, remain available in the hours before the show in case something needed attention, and then, after the audience was gone, get everything packed and loaded back up and settle up with the promoter so they could leave in time to get to the next venue—where they did it all over again. Nine months of the year. "There are very few promoters who actually took an interest in that whole time you were there. Peter was one of those guys," Arlo said. "From the moment [we] got there, he was there. He was there with us backstage at one in the afternoon. The show didn't start until eight and the catering didn't begin until three, but he was there anyway. And I love that about him. He took an interest in all of what it takes to do a show, rather than just the promotion of the show itself."

Arlo was also impressed with Peter's ability to bring him to venues in towns he didn't know existed before, where he ended up playing to packed houses of appreciative concertgoers. That became particularly important and useful when he found himself booked for a big show in Chicago with several days or even a week or two before the next big show somewhere west of the Mississippi River. Peter helped him transform what might other-wise have been an abundance of downtime into paying gigs. "He made a tour out of a stop," Arlo said. "And so instead of calling up Peter for a date in Milwaukee, I'd say, 'I've got two weeks. Can you put together something in the area that will occupy that time?' And he'd say 'Yeah,' and he would do it. And the shows were great."

Peter vividly remembers one Arlo show in 1994 involving a note from an audience member. Not infrequently, a concertgoer will try to pass something to the artist at a show—a letter with a request, a declaration of appreciation, or a material gift of some kind. Whenever possible, Peter preferred to intercept those offerings before they got to their intended recipient. If the handwritten messages weren't sealed, he'd read them

This picture of Arlo Guthrie (left), Peter, and John Prine (right) was taken at a show in Colorado. Peter wasn't the promoter—he was just a guy who came to see his friends play.

before passing them along. The last thing he wanted to do was upset an act before they went on stage.

But this particular note wasn't upsetting. The writer explained that she had intended to come to the show with her husband, but in the interval between them buying the tickets and the show itself, he had died. That show, two months after she'd become a widow, was her first night out since his funeral. Would it be possible, she asked, for Arlo to perform "Amazing Grace"?

In the 1980s and early 1990s, Arlo had closed all his shows with the song, and Peter speculated that the woman had seen one of those shows with her husband. But Arlo hadn't performed the song in years. Peter handed the note to Arlo before he went on, then headed out into the house to watch the show. Near the end of the night, Arlo addressed the audience. "I want to dedicate this song to someone in the audience because it means something to them, and here it is," he said, before launching into "Amazing Grace." The woman in the audience audibly gasped. It was the perfect dedication—an intimate gesture, even in front of a crowd, directly from Arlo to his fan. Peter wasn't sure whether Arlo knew he'd read the woman's letter, but at the end of the night, he made sure to tell him, "That was really special."

By that time, Peter's love for Arlo even exceeded his devotion to the Packers on Sundays. On one off day between a bunch of Arlo dates, Peter was settling in to watch Green Bay play the Minnesota Vikings—a long-standing rivalry. The game had just started when the phone rang. "Peter! It's Arlo," he said. "Hey, we're going to the zoo. Do you want to come with us?" It was an offer Peter would have turned down flat from anyone else. But he turned off the game, got the motorcycle out of the garage, and met up with Arlo, his son, Abe, and a few members of his touring crew at the zoo. Afterward, they all went out for Thai food. Arlo and Abe ordered the spiciest things on the menu, while Peter got his Massaman curry at a solidly medium spice level.

On January 27, 2000, Arlo and Peter were in the audience at Shank Hall—an unusual part of the venue for Arlo to find himself in. On this occasion, the headliner was his daughter, twenty-year-old Sarah Lee Guthrie. The men sat together at one of the round tables by the sound board. Arlo's phone was aimed toward the stage. On the other end of the phone, in Florida, was Jackie Guthrie. Arlo wanted to make sure his wife was as present as she could be to experience their youngest's first show outside of the family's home state of Massachusetts.

That Arlo Guthrie—who could have had his choice of pretty much any stage in any state for his daughter's show—had asked Peter if she could play Shank Hall, and that Peter's immediate response was "Of course!" says everything about their relationship. In that moment, Arlo was simply a caring father making a deliberate and informed choice. "I knew that Sarah Lee wanted to play," he said, "and she had to start somewhere. And there was nowhere I felt better about than putting her in [Peter's] hands, because I knew the environment was going to be as easy an entrance into the world of music as could be. I felt like Sarah Lee could be herself and she could get up on stage and sing her songs and the venue would be the perfect place." Peter, who regretted not having children of his own only when it snowed and there was no one to shovel the driveway, had never said no to Arlo and would never say no to another Guthrie.

Peter's attendance at Arlo's shows wasn't limited to the ones he promoted. If Arlo was doing a show in a neighboring state, or if Peter was on vacation in a place where Arlo was playing, he bought a ticket and caught the show. The year 2008 was a bad one for Peter. His father had been diagnosed with cancer that January, and he died in March. Then, in July, his fifteen-year-old dog, Sammy, died.

"I've just got to get away," Peter told his mother, who, as always, understood. He packed the saddlebags on his Harley for the three-hundred-mile trip from Milwaukee to Bayfield, where Arlo was performing at Big Top Chautauqua. Peter's friends Paul and Karen LeSage would meet him there and join him at the show, then he'd spend the night on the foldout couch of their RV before heading home. He was in Bayfield when he got the call—Mike Wallander, his former roommate and high school buddy, had died.

"I was just devastated," Peter remembered. "I mean, within four months, my dad, my dog, and my best friend had died. If I were a country artist, I would have had a number one hit record, but being away from home, where I like to be, and to have my best friend die?" The only thing that made the distance away from home bearable was that Mike had liked Arlo, too, and had seen him perform on multiple occasions. After the show,

Seventeen years after her Shank Hall show, Sarah Lee Guthrie (left) shared the stage with her father, Arlo (right), at Milwaukee's Pabst Theater. PHOTO BY EROL REYAL

Peter and Arlo spent some time together. "I talked to him about Mike and it was so good being with him," Peter said.

That the feeling was mutual was brought home to him during a moment at a subsequent Arlo show, a moment Peter treasures. He was standing backstage with Sarah Lee when Arlo thanked Peter from the stage. Sarah Lee, responding to Peter's expression of surprise, said, "You're like family. You're like a Guthrie to us."

11

Only Love

In the early days of his promoting career, when Peter had booked John Prine to perform at UWM's Wisconsin Room in October of 1986, their interactions had been cordial, but strictly business-related. And as they continued to work together, things remained that way—at least as far as Peter was concerned. He dealt with Prine's booking agent, Prine showed up at the venue (or venues, if Peter had booked a series of multicity dates), Prine did the show(s), Peter paid the tour manager, the Prine caravan moved on, and that was the last contact they'd have until the cycle repeated itself. But after several years, their relationship started to shift.

In 1991, when Mitchell Drosin became Prine's new tour manager, he knew he was stepping into an organization with an established culture and routines. In one early meeting with his new boss, Drosin remembered, the conversation turned to making sure he had the right contacts in various cities. Mitchell was checking that he had everything in order. "So, we use SFX in Milwaukee, right?" he'd asked Prine. Mitchell was so sure of the response that he'd all but written SFX—the giant concert promoter that would later be sold to Clear Channel and then spun off as Live Nation—on the pad in his hand before asking. It was definitely already there in his mind. Which is why he was not prepared for his new boss's answer. "No, no," Prine responded. "We use this guy named Peter Jest."

Mitchell managed to utter a bewildered, "What?"

"He owns Shank Hall and he's promoted me forever," Prine said. "I'm not screwing him. He is my promoter in all Wisconsin. I don't want to hear [anything more] about it. So, if there's any shows you want to do [in Wisconsin], you're going to contact Peter."

Peter was privy to none of this. But the relationship growing between him and Prine made itself more apparent after a show at Milwaukee's Marcus Center on July 14, 1995. It was part of Prine's *Lost Dogs* tour. Peter had booked about six or seven shows for Prine over the course of nine years, and he'd established the same routine with Prine that he had with most other national acts he booked—he made sure the artists had what they needed, then he left them alone. Outside of show-related matters, conversations mainly consisted of polite small talk.

But that night, after the show was over and Peter had settled up with Mitchell, something unexpected happened. "As John is walking out of the Marcus Center," Peter remembered, "he turns around and says, 'Hey, if you ever come to Nashville, give me a call and I'll show you around,' and I thought, *Wow. That was really cool.*"

From then on, once the business portion of a show was completed, things between Peter and John were more social. After one show, the two of them and Mitchell got into a sports-related discussion, and someone brought up Michael Jordan, the legendary Chicago Bulls shooting guard. Prine, a Chicago native, was a big Jordan fan. So, he added, were his three young sons.

John Prine and Peter hanging out in Green Bay, circa 2000.

"Well, I can get tickets," Peter told him. "Come up to Milwaukee some-time and we'll go to a Bucks game." In January of 1998, John did just that. Through Peter's long-standing relationship with Miller Brewing, he was able to secure a suite for the game. And because he was familiar with John's tour rider—which, because John was a routine-oriented guy, changed very little over the years they worked together—he knew what snacks to order. Peter also knew to make sure that, in addition to beer, there was vodka, ginger ale, and lime—the ingredients for John's preferred drink, which he had dubbed the "Handsome Johnny."

When it was time to go to the game, he met John and the boys in the lobby of the Hyatt Regency on Third Street. It was a short three-block walk to the Bradley Center. After twelve years of booking Prine shows, Peter had a good sense of John Prine the artist. Now, on a social outing with his friend John Prine, there was no band, no fanfare. It was just a boy's night out—a dad doing something special with his young sons. The cold weather wasn't a big deal for John, who'd grown up in Chicago. His boys, though, were Nashville natives and not used to Milwaukee winters.

Peter watched as John knelt in front of his sons, making certain that Jody, Jack, and Tommy had their coats zipped all the way to the top. He checked that their hats were over their ears and looked for gaps between their mit-tens and their sleeves. On the way to the game, John and Peter held the kids' hands as they crossed Fourth Street. Once inside the suite, John tended to the boys while Peter tended bar. When he handed John his drink, John handed it back. "Oh, no," he said. "I don't want to drink in front of the boys."

The final score was 96-86; the Bulls won. On their way out, someone walking past them did a double take: "Hey! It's John Prine!" That observant basketball fan was the only person to notice him all night.

A year later, two days after a show at Milwaukee's Riverside Theater on June 10, 1999, Peter had the opportunity to meet another member of John's family. John and Mitchell invited Peter down to Cicero, Illinois, where John (along with Hootie and the Blowfish, Lucinda Williams, Elvis Costello, Van Morrison, Shane MacGowan, and Taj Mahal) was performing at the Guinness Fleadh. As they were leaving the hotel in downtown Chicago in advance of strolling the festival grounds at the Chicago Motor Speedway, Mitchell pointed out a pretty, dark-haired woman standing in a small cluster of people.

"There's Fiona," he said. They walked over and stood quietly until the woman pulled away to greet Mitchell. "Fiona, this is Peter Jest," he said. Peter, expecting a polite hello from John's wife, instead found himself swept up in a warm hug. When she pulled away, Fiona was smiling up at him as if he were a friend she hadn't seen in too long. "I've heard so much about you!" she said.

By this time, Mitchell and Peter had established their own connection. "When we came to Wisconsin, it was like seeing your long-lost brother," Mitchell said of Peter, "because besides the business end of it, we all got along really, really well. It was always super easy, and we knew each other's habits, good and bad."

One of Mitchell's favorite Peter stories is the one about the party box. Mitchell and John were in Massachusetts prior to a Wisconsin tour stop. After his shows, John liked to take whatever food was left in his dressing room back to where he was spending the night. "So, I actually had an empty cardboard box on the rider," Mitchell said, "because I could never find a cardboard box at a gig and it was driving me nuts." John wanted to leave the venue as soon as his show ended at 11:00 so that he could catch the cold open of *Saturday Night Live* from his hotel room. Before he left that night, he gave Mitchell a status report. "The party box is packed," John said. "It's right outside my dressing room."

After settling up with the promoter and taking care of whatever else required his attention, Mitchell went to get the box so he could, as usual,

Peter—who has an excellent memory, especially for dates—doesn't remember when John Prine wrote this note, but that says a lot about their relationship. Peter does recall that it was about one of the events he and John attended together—a Cubs, White Sox, Bulls, or Nashville Predators game.

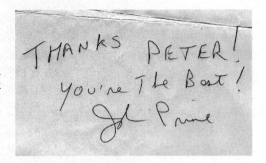

bring it to John's room. The garment bag was by the door, but the box was gone. Mitchell called John to see if he'd taken it. "No," John told him. "I left it right there."

"I'm telling you," Mitchell said. "It's not there." Had the cleaning staff taken it? Had it found its way onto one of the tour vehicles? The drivers hadn't seen it. Mitchell went looking for the promoter, but he'd taken off. Mitchell called him.

"By any chance," he asked, "did you take a box from outside John's dressing room?"

"Yeah," the promoter said, "he left all this stuff and I didn't want it to go to waste."

Mitchell explained the situation. But the promoter, an hour down the road, said he wasn't coming back.

"And it has John's alcohol in it, and it's one in the morning. I can't get booze," Mitchell recalled. It goes without saying that that was the last time that promoter did a John Prine show. It was a long night for Mitchell, who was reduced to buying individual shots from the bar and pouring them into a bottle.

The story traveled faster than the act, and Peter heard about it before they arrived in Milwaukee. When they got to the venue and Mitchell went looking for the box, he found it—with a chain and lock attached. "His name is perfect," Mitchell said, "the Jest jester."

It was 2010 and Karen Hayden was pretty sure she was done with husbands. Like John Prine, she had begun a relationship with Peter as a strictly business arrangement. She and Tracy Roe, Shank's bar manager, had been working together as bartenders at Mader's, a local German restaurant, when Tracy offered her a waitressing job at the club. In late 1996, when her daughter, Elise, was six months old, Karen began working there regularly. The hours meshed well with her other job, directing a church choir. It was just the right amount of part-time work for a full-time parent. When she and her then-husband moved to the East Side, not far from where Peter lived, she began interacting more frequently with her boss.

"If he didn't want to go into the club right away, he'd ask me to come by and pick up the change or the paychecks and bring them in, because we were usually there half an hour to an hour before doors in order to set up," Karen remembered.

After that had become a semiregular occurrence, Peter asked if she'd be willing to walk his dog Sammy on the occasions when he was out of town doing shows. Peter gave her a set of keys to his house. Over the course of various conversations, he discovered Karen was a New Orleans Saints fan. By then, it was 2000. Her marriage was over; she was also a single parent on a budget. When Peter found out that Karen didn't have cable, he'd occasionally invite her over so she could catch a Saints game. It was a comfortable situation, in part because of an unspoken but understood dynamic: they were work friends enjoying a common pastime outside of the office. Plus, Peter usually had a girlfriend, and Karen wasn't really interested in dating anyone.

Then, in 2006, Karen got a full-time job as an administrative assistant at Children's Hospital of Wisconsin and moved out of the neighborhood. She continued her weekend gig directing the church choir, but Shank Hall—and Peter—became less of a regular presence in her life. If someone was out of town or there was an especially big show that required extra help, Peter would ask her to fill in if she was available. She'd also show up if an act she liked was playing at Shank—Ike Reilly, Rasputina, and Tina and the B-Sides were her favorites. And then, in 2010, her phone rang. She'd just had to put her cat down due to illness, and it was Peter, calling to tell her he was sorry and to see if she was okay. A couple of months later, he called again and asked if she wanted to hang out. They went out for dinner.

"He'd just broken up with somebody, and he was bummed," she said. As they were heading to their respective cars, he asked if she'd be interested in doing something again. She said she would. Maybe a movie, she suggested. And then, Peter asked Karen a question that landed like the punchline of a really good joke: "Have you ever thought about us dating or anything?"

When she stopped laughing, she looked him over and told the truth. "Well," she said, "you've always been my [redacted] boss, but if you want to hang out, we can see if anything happens. But let's just take it slowly."

Karen was pretty sure nothing would come of it. She was wrong. Their first date was at a comedy show in Madison. Steve Martin was performing; Peter was copromoting. After the show, his copromoter Don Kronberg insisted on taking a picture of Peter and Karen with Martin standing between them—one of the relatively rare times Peter has been photographed with one of his acts at a show.

As Peter and Karen spent more time together, she started to piece together a more complete version of the guy formerly known as her [redacted] boss. She had already known that, as she put it, "his jeans are gonna be all ratty on the bottom and his shirts are going to have stains on them and his hair is not going to be kempt." But the guy whose wardrobe mostly consisted of John Prine tour shirts, jeans, and sneakers also knew how and when to dress up—sort of. One Sunday not long after they started

Peter's copromoter, Don Kronberg, didn't want him to pass up the opportunity to get a picture with the actor Steve Martin (center), especially because Peter had brought Karen (left) on a first date to the show.

dating, Karen was singing a solo at Bethany Calvary United Methodist Church, where she led the choir. Instead of going to Our Redeemer with his mother that week, Peter surprised Karen by attending the service, dressed in a button-down shirt and slacks. "His shirt was inside out," Karen recalled. "Luckily it was kind of a dark color, so you couldn't really tell."

She also learned about his eating habits, which did not include a lot of green things. About three months after they began dating, Peter invited Karen to be his plus-one at his nephew Benjamin's wedding. "Our plates came out," she remembered, "and Peter looked at his plate and said, 'What are those? Green beans?' And I said, 'No, that's . . . yeah. Those are green beans.' And then he ate them. . . . I said, 'Did you like your green beans?' He said, 'Yes.' I said, 'Good. Now we know that you like asparagus.'"

He said he had known something was up, but he trusted her anyway. It was another in a line of things she was learning—and liking—about Peter. He was a devoted son and brother who lavished attention on his pets, some of them rescues who would otherwise have been euthanized. He was a generous friend and a boss whose high—though occasionally unrealistic—expectations of his staff sometimes made it easy to miss how deeply he trusted, relied on, and cared about them. And there was an ease between them, born of how long they'd known each other.

Peter proposed on March 7, 2011. Karen said yes. And Peter Jest, concert promoter, became Peter Jest, wedding planner. Except for choosing the music for the ceremony, Karen turned everything over to Peter. "He's very focused about what he needs to get done," Karen said. "And he's detail-oriented, and . . . very much 'This is what I'm doing now, and now you're in my way, and I'm in charge.' And if anything goes wrong, I'm going to be blamed. And so, that's why, when we got married, it was like, 'Fine. You can plan it all!' . . . So yeah, it turns out that having a concert promoter as a wedding planner is not a bad deal."

The event, attended by three hundred, was a who's who of local music royalty. Dave Luhrssen was the best man, and radio personality Steve Amann was a groomsman. Semi-Twang was the wedding band. The attendees included promoters and musicians such as Bob Babisch, Randy McElrath, Leslie West, Joe Balistreri, and Ron Paskin. Musicians Robin Pluer and Paul Cebar joined with Semi-Twang to make an R&B Cadets reunion at the reception, which was held at Bullwinkle's in Brookfield.

Peter's old business partner Bob Weidenbaum and his wife, Kathy, flew in from Arizona. Jerry Lima, a close friend and music agent, came from California. Steve Sperling from the Barrymore, Madison-based promoter Tag Evers, and Madison-based agent Jeff Laramie also attended, and there was a table's worth of Peter's classmates from Milwaukee Lutheran. John and Fiona Prine, who couldn't be present, sent the remaining six or seven items on the couple's wedding registry.

Peter's approximately ten-minute speech that day remains the longest solo of his life, which he acknowledged in its opening lines. "I never get to speak, and I'm paying for this anyway," he said, stopping to let the laughter and applause die back, "so I might as well get my money's worth."

About his relationship with Karen, he said: "We really fell in love after a while and realized that we really were meant for each other. . . . Many of the reasons were her love of God, family, music, animals, football, hockey."

Peter also addressed one of the big questions people who knew him well were wondering about. It wasn't a secret that children weren't his favorite variety of human, and it wasn't a secret that Karen had a daughter. "I don't have kids and I don't like noisy kids—how was I going to get along with Elise? I'm happy to report that we get along great.

Peter and Karen after their wedding ceremony on June 23, 2012.

Peter with his best man, Dave Luhrssen.

I always liked Elise when she was growing up—there's a picture of her sleeping on my dog in the back seat of my car. . . . I'm very happy that she's my stepdaughter."

He thanked the friends who were helping with sound and pictures, and he explained why he'd asked Semi-Twang to play his wedding.

> There are certainly a lot of great bands and people that I could have had. . . . Mark Shurilla and the Greatest Hits, Paul Cebar and the Milwaukeeans, and other bands, but Semi-Twang and me have a unique relationship. I bothered John Sieger and the rest of the guys for years to get back together, and they did for the twentieth anniversary of Shank Hall, and because of that they've stayed together as a band, put out a great CD called *Wages of Sin*, and in every interview they do, they credit me for getting them back together. They thanked me on the record. They gave me a nice big plaque. . . . It's nice to be involved with a band on that level, where they appreciate you, and when I talked to Karen, that was the only choice.

He also addressed the reason he hadn't considered holding the reception at Shank Hall, which generated laughter, along with applause from the table where his staff sat. "I don't want my friends working," he explained. "And plus, I'd probably yell at them too much."

Peter concluded the speech with a tribute to friends and family who had died, including his father (he wore Marvin's military dog tags to the ceremony and reception); his closest friend, Mike Wallander; and most recently, Mark Shurilla, whose death a month prior had shocked Milwaukee's music community. Peter's last words were an overview of the music to follow: "We're going to start the night tonight, after I speak, with two wedding songs from friends of mine who aren't dead: John Prine, 'This Love Is Real,' and Arlo Guthrie, 'My Love.' And right after that, we're going to have a punk polka song by Mark Shurilla and the Black Holes called 'Blitzkrieg Over Kenosha.' And since this is Wisconsin, and it's polka, I want everyone to get out there and polka and right after that, Semi-Twang will [play]."

One week after the wedding, on June 30, 2012, Karen and Peter found themselves at a John Prine show at Presentation Hall in Rochester, Minnesota. From their obstructed-view seats—behind the merch table looking toward the closed theater doors—Karen and Mitchell Drosin could hear the performance pretty clearly. Karen had been Peter's wife for exactly a week; Mitchell had been John's tour manager and booking agent for more than two decades. Together, they'd arranged the cardboard boxes of T-shirts, sweatshirts, and CDs so they'd be within easy reach when the show let out and memento-seeking audience members headed their way. Among the items on display was *Lost Dogs & Mixed Blessings*, John's 1995 release featuring "This Love Is Real," the track Peter had chosen for his first dance with Karen.

"It was near the end of the show, and I was doing stuff," Karen remembered. "And then, all of a sudden, I heard him say 'Peter and Karen.' So, I knew he was doing something. I wasn't sure exactly what it was, but it was obviously that he was dedicating his song to us."

The song was "Only Love," from John's 1984 album, *Aimless Love*. John had sung it at his own wedding to Fiona in 1996. Peter preserved the moment on his and Karen's wedding video, where it serves as the opening sequence. Over a still image of Peter in his wedding finery, extending a hand to Karen as she exits the limousine transporting them from the church to the reception venue, is a perfectly in-tune arpeggiated D-major chord, then Prine speaking. "I'd like to sing this song for the fella that promoted the show, Peter Jest," he says. "Peter's from Milwaukee, and he just got married last week, and I wasn't able to attend the wedding. But Peter, I want to wish you and Karen the best, and this song's for you."

The transition to married life was easy. Years of knowing each other in so many different contexts gave Peter and Karen a sense of familiarity and comfort. Their stage of life also worked to their advantage. There was no need to talk about whether they wanted to have children, or where to live, or about career choices and advancement. Marriage also provided each with something tangible and life-improving. In Karen's case, it was a house—Peter owned one, and she didn't. For Peter, it was Karen's full-time job with benefits. As her husband, he was able to get on her health insurance plan. It became a trope in their marriage. Peter's line was "I've got to work hard to keep you in luxury." Karen's was "I have to work hard to keep you in pharmaceuticals."

The health insurance turned out to be a very good thing, and not just because of Peter's asthma and allergies. In April of 2019, Karen was diagnosed with breast cancer. John Prine, who was a two-time cancer survivor by then, was in a hospital in Nashville for an unrelated issue the same day Karen started treatment in Milwaukee.

"We took a little video to just wish her well," Fiona said of the greeting she shot of John, in his hospital bed, singing and saying hello. Fiona sent a care package that included candles and essential oils from Thistle Farms, a Nashville-area nonprofit for female survivors of prostitution, addiction, and trafficking.

Fiona had started accompanying John, Mitchell, and the band on the road around 2014. "I thought he needed to be with somebody, with family, on the road," she said. Then, when John's manager of forty-two years, Al Bunetta, died ten days after being hospitalized for cancer in 2015, Fiona took on that role as well.

Fiona noticed how John looked forward to being in Wisconsin on tour. "It was always a special thing when he was going to do that run," she said, "because it was for Peter, with Peter. John just loved those shows, because . . . Peter knew him well and knew what he liked and what he didn't like. John had, I would say . . . a couple of close friends and a lot of acquaintances, and we're really alike in that way. We don't have to see all our friends all the time in order to have that kind of bond and that friendship and the genuine kind of caring. . . . So, when he would see Peter, they'd take up just where they left off."

By the late 2010s, John and his band were playing approximately ninety dates a year, which added up to them spending about twice that amount of time on the road. John's tour rider rarely varied from venue to venue, so Fiona picked up on the Wisconsin variation pretty quickly. "I started noticing that every time we went up around the Milwaukee area, there was always a sheet cake after the show," she said. "Somebody broke the news to me [and I realized] that, 'Oh, this was . . . part of the rider, that Peter's mom would make a big sheet cake and pretend it was John's birthday.'"

That was partially right. It was always *someone*'s birthday, though not necessarily John's. That was, Mitchell said, so John wouldn't be embarrassed by the cake and accompanying ice cream. The origin story goes back to a mid-nineties phone call between Mitchell and Peter in advance of a

Milwaukee show. They had been talking shop when the conversation turned to food. That John had a sweet tooth was no secret. On the road, he loved to find a local Dairy Queen, and he always liked cake and ice cream after a show. Sourcing food was one of the many components of Mitchell's job as tour manager, though he would also take over booking for John in 2015. Finding ice cream on the road was easy, but John especially liked yellow cake with chocolate frosting, which was more of a hit-or-miss situation. Mitchell was lamenting the difficulty of finding good yellow cake on the road when Peter said, "Oh, my mom makes it." So, after that show, John and the band enjoyed what would be the first of twenty-five years' worth of yellow cakes with chocolate icing made by Kathryn Jest.

One of the last cakes she made for John, in October of 2018, traveled to Nashville, where he was touring behind what turned out to be his final album, *The Tree of Forgiveness*. The October 6 show was close to his birthday on the tenth, and Peter arranged to fly down and surprise him. "When I got there," Peter remembered, "[John] was sound checking, and Mitchell said, 'Go talk to him,' so during sound check, I walked out with the cake, and he turns around and looks at me, and without missing a beat, says, 'What am I, in Wisconsin?'"

John Prine and his band on stage at the Riverside Theater in April of 2018. This was his last Milwaukee show. PHOTO BY KELSEA MCCULLOCH, COURTESY OF PABST THEATER GROUP

Six months earlier, John, Fiona, and Mitchell had been at the Riverside Theater for Milwaukee's stop on the *Tree of Forgiveness* tour. Kathryn had baked her usual cake for after the show, and during sound check, Peter presented each of the Prines with a gift. Fiona got a dozen roses. Jody, Tommy, and Jack each got a Milwaukee Bucks Giannis Antetokounmpo jersey. But John's gift was one of a kind—something Peter had learned about John while listening to him promote his new album. Someone had wanted to know the name of John's favorite cartoon character. His response was instant: "Foghorn Leghorn."

Within seconds of hearing that answer, Peter was on his computer, emailing his cousin Spike Brandt in Los Angeles, who'd spent years working as a Warner Brothers animator and drawing Looney Toons characters before going out on his own. "Hey!" Peter wrote: "Can you do me a favor? John Prine's favorite cartoon character is Foghorn Leghorn. Could you make something up? Thanks!"

The cake and the roses, of course, are long gone. The Bucks jerseys have been laundered multiple times. But, the Foghorn Leghorn drawings? John had them framed, and they're still hanging on the wall in the main-floor bathroom of his and Fiona's house.

Peter commissioned his cousin, artist Spike Brandt, to create this drawing of Foghorn Leghorn as a gift for John Prine.
ARTWORK BY
SPIKE BRANDT

12

Hope Springs Eternal

Throughout the 1990s and 2000s, Peter developed his working relationships and friendships with artists like Kottke, Redbone, Guthrie, and Prine—all of whom came through Wisconsin fairly regularly. He had also begun working regularly with two other acts—Canadian singer-songwriter Gordon Lightfoot and pianist George Winston. Peter's relationship with Lightfoot had started as a one-off at the Barrymore in April of 2001, but soon he was doing with Gordon and his band what he'd been doing for decades with Guthrie and Prine: putting together multicity tours around the state. Gordon's band and tour staff had been working together for decades. Gordon and Peter immediately forged a relationship based on their mutual love of hockey and John Prine. Soon, they were catching each other up on the minutiae of their lives between the Wisconsin shows. Getting to know George, a solo artist, was even easier for Peter. They were both cat lovers, and each had the rare ability to remember the smallest details of previous shows.

Peter was also making plans to book his biggest acts yet. On February 21, 2009, he stared at the monitor, rereading the draft of his email one last time. He looked past the monitor and up at Echo, who peered back from his usual spot on the branch that stretched from the edge of his perch and into the sunroom, which was open to Peter's office. Then, he took a deep breath, hitting "Send" as he exhaled. He hoped he was striking the right tone. A day earlier, he'd emailed Robert Kory, Leonard Cohen's manager. Kory had referred him to Elliott Lefko, a vice president at AEG Goldenvoice, whom Peter copied on his response. Lefko was in charge of promoting Cohen's upcoming tour.

"My name is Peter Jest," he'd written. "I have been promoting concerts in theatres around Wisconsin and Illinois for over 25 years. I also own a club in Milwaukee: Shank Hall. Congratulations on getting the Leonard Cohen tour. Would you be interested in adding May 7 at the Milwaukee [Theatre]? I do not believe he has ever played here and I believe we could do very well with the Milwaukee and Madison area crowds. You obviously could do the show yourself at the Milwaukee Theatre but I would like to be a partner on the date as I feel I could really be a help in promoting the show."

Lefko's two-line, eleven-word response arrived the next day: "Let's see how the tour goes. Email me next month, please."

Peter's idea to try to bring a big performer like Leonard Cohen to Milwaukee—where he hadn't played for a very long time—had been partly inspired by his friend and fellow venue owner Leslie West. Way back in 1992, the same year Peter left Cellar Door, Leslie and her husband, Joe Balistreri, had purchased the Eagles Club building just west of downtown Milwaukee. Their home number was unlisted, making the call from a stranger with an axe to grind about a business issue an especially unwelcome surprise. Peter wasn't expecting anything good to come of the call, either. He just wanted the new owner of the building to know he wouldn't appreciate being shut out of one of his regular show venues. He'd had a good relationship with the previous owners of the club on Twenty-Fifth and Wisconsin. He was pretty sure the new owners weren't going to work with outside promoters.

"Once I told him he could come in here any time he wanted to do a show he said, 'Oh!' and changed his tune," Leslie said. "It started out as a testy conversation, and once he realized he could do whatever he wanted here, he was fine."

Over a decade later, their daily conversations ranged from what they were going to have for dinner to the types of things they said aloud only to the safest people in their lives. When Peter married Karen, Leslie had been in the wedding party. "Leslie is such a creative person," Peter said. "She could write a book that would be much more interesting than mine. Once, when she couldn't get an act . . . she found out what the manager's favorite beer was and sent the manager, like, a hundred cases of his favorite beer and got the date."

Witnessing the thoughtfulness Leslie brought to her work, Peter understood: no matter who they are, people want to feel as if they matter. And in a business that had become increasingly corporate, with Live Nation (which would later own Ticketmaster) and AEG (which would later own AXS) competing for the majority of live concert and festival business, solo promoters and independent venue owners needed to be creative, persistent, and daring. Leslie was Peter's friend, but she was also an inspiration.

Sometime around the end of 2008, Peter got reflective. Shank Hall was self-sufficient and regularly hosted a rotating roster of up-and-coming acts, local favorites, and classic artists. He loved his ACG regulars—John Prine, Arlo Guthrie, Gordon Lightfoot, George Winston, the Violent Femmes, and Jesse Cook among them—and he consistently got other shows through his relationships with agents (and, in some cases, close friends) like Steve Martin, Jerry Lima, Elizabeth Rush, and Brian Hill. But he needed—and wanted—a new and different kind of challenge.

At the same time, and for very different reasons, Leonard Cohen had also gotten reflective. In 2007, he was in the aftermath of having discovered that his longtime manager had stolen upwards of $8 million from him. At a work session for songs that eventually became part of the album *Old Ideas*, he told his longtime collaborator Sharon Robinson, "I think I'm going to have to go on tour. My bank accounts are empty. I went to the ATM and I couldn't get any money out." The first leg of Cohen's tour, from 2008 into 2009, covered Europe and Australia. The date Peter requested in May was one of a pair of unscheduled dates between two nights at the Chicago Theater and a Detroit show at the Fox Theater. After asking Peter to wait for a month to see how the first leg of the tour went, Lefko ultimately gave him a definitive answer: the tour was full.

Several years later, Peter tried again, this time for a November 24, 2012, date. The situation was similar to 2009—Cohen had two off days between two Chicago shows and a single Detroit date. On June 29, he sent another email to Robert Kory. This time, Kory told Peter he would discuss it with Lefko and asked Peter to send Lefko an offer.

Peter sent the offer on July 1, the morning after John Prine had sung "Only Love" in honor of his wedding to Karen. "I just came back from promoting John Prine in Rochester on Saturday," he wrote.

John Prine is my main act that I promote in the Midwest. Mitchell Drosin speaks very highly of you. I have asked a few times about avails for Leonard Cohen and you have responded that nothing is available—but I can be an aggressive promoter for an act I believe in. . . . I do not believe Leonard Cohen has played in Wisconsin since the 1970s if at all. I feel this would be a tremendous success as I can market the show state wide with an emphasis on Madison as a major fan market. I know you may have other plans for this date or may want 2 days off but as you know Leonard Cohen is a rare musical genius and I do not know if I or his Wisconsin fans will get too many more chances to see him in the future if we can't make a date happen this year. Please let me know if there is anything I can do to get this to happen.

Lefko's response to Kory came a day later: "I think we should copromote with this guy [Peter] for this one date and he will market." In August, Lefko wrote to let Peter know, "If it doesn't happen there will be one more opportunity on another leg. So stay in touch."

Peter's next email was a check-in, letting Lefko know that the November date was still on hold with the Milwaukee Theatre. Lefko wrote back that it didn't look good and that they should revisit things at the end of the month. He also offered Peter a pair of complimentary tickets "for Chicago or somewhere on the tour." Peter thanked him for the tickets, but said no. He wasn't ready to give up on his dream of seeing his first Leonard Cohen show in his own city.

On November 19, Peter and his friend Jim Hoehn headed up to Eau Claire's State Theatre for the second of three Lindsey Buckingham shows Peter was promoting. The singer-guitarist had already done a tour for his most recent solo release, *Seeds We Sow*, and now he was doing more solo shows before going out with his former band, Fleetwood Mac, for a reunion tour. Hoehn, a singer-songwriter with a day job—sports reporter for the *Milwaukee Journal Sentinel*—was coming up to catch the show and visit relatives.

Buckingham's stage setup included a 9-by-12-foot Oriental rug. Someone in the artist's traveling entourage had forgotten it in South Milwaukee, so Peter and Jim's first stop on the way to Eau Claire was a

This photo of Peter, Lindsey Buckingham (center), and Karen (right) was taken in Madison a few nights before Peter found out he'd gotten his much-sought-after Leonard Cohen date.

ten-mile detour in the opposite direction to retrieve the carpet, which they managed to successfully muscle into Peter's Toyota Yaris. It was a tight fit; the rug stretched from the windshield to the back window, making for an obstructed view from both the passenger's and driver's seats.

At the theater, they unloaded the carpet and laid it out on stage. Peter set himself up where he always did—close enough to be available if needed and far enough to be out of the way. At some venues, a vacant office would be designated for the promoter; sometimes it was just a table in a hallway. At 6:25 p.m., about ninety minutes before the show started, Peter's cell phone rang. Elliott Lefko was calling.

"Peter," he said, "so, do you think this will really work?"

"Yes, Elliott. Leonard Cohen has not been here in thirty-eight years. I have the marketing plan all sketched out. This'll do really well, it will be great, and you'll have my full attention as a small promoter. I will be on this twenty-four seven."

"Okay. We were thinking about doing Columbus, Ohio, but we're going to do Milwaukee with you instead."

Peter hung up. Jim was looking at him. Peter told him the news. "You can't tell a soul," he said. They stood alongside the stage watching Lindsey Buckingham sing his moody tunes and work his quick-fingered guitar magic. After settling up and walking Lindsey back to his car, Peter and Jim spent the drive home (sans carpet) processing the news.

Three days later, at the big Jest family Thanksgiving dinner, Peter and Karen shared aloud their gratitude over celebrating their first holiday as a married couple. Peter's thanks for having secured a Leonard Cohen tour date were offered up silently. He kept the news contained within a very tight circle. Karen knew because she was his wife. Jim knew because he'd been there at the moment Peter found out and Peter wouldn't be able to contain news that big and fresh for a five-hour drive. Three other Milwaukeeans were told in advance of the public announcement.

Dave Luhrssen was one, partly because of his and Peter's personal relationship but mainly because, as the arts and entertainment editor of the *Shepherd Express*, he would need enough lead time to assign or write a story to run in conjunction with the public announcement. For the same business-related reason, Peter told Piet Levy, the music and entertainment reporter for the *Milwaukee Journal Sentinel*, and Tom Crawford, the general manager at WMSE. Peter knew he could trust all three to stay quiet.

On Wednesday, January 9, 2013, the press release announcing a second North American leg of the *Old Ideas* world tour was sent to media outlets. Piet Levy's piece announcing the show in Milwaukee ran in that day's *Journal Sentinel*. It noted:

> Cohen's last Milwaukee concert was Feb. 25, 1975, at what is now the Marcus Center for the Performing Arts. In the period since then, there were 15 years where Cohen didn't tour at all. He returned to the road in 2008, in part because a former manager had allegedly made off with Cohen's money while the songwriter was living in a Buddhist monastery. In the meantime, local concert promoter and Cohen fan Peter Jest, who runs the east side music venue Shank Hall, had begun a years-long quest with Cohen's manager and tour promoter AEG Live to bring Cohen back to Milwaukee.

Within hours of the announcement, people were already preparing to attend. On a Leonard Cohen fan forum, one fan asked about the Milwaukee venue. Another responded: "Milwaukee Theatre is a fantastic venue. It is the old Milwaukee Auditorium that they renovated in 2001. About 4,000 seat capacity. Very nice place in downtown Milwaukee."

Between the public announcement and the moment Cohen and his band took the stage, Peter needed to handle a host of logistics. First was the tickets. Peter received an email listing the dates when tickets would be made available to the general public. Prior to that date, members of select groups would each be able to buy up to eight tickets to the show—Leonard's fan club (three days before the general public), American Express cardholders (two days before), and AEG's past ticket-buyers (one day before). In addition to ticket sales, Peter also managed Cohen's requests regarding the media coverage of the show. There would be no interviews with Cohen, who had made it clear to his management that he didn't want to meet anyone in advance of or after shows. His priority was saving everything he had for the three hours he spent on stage.

A story in the *Journal Sentinel* revealed that Peter had spent a lot longer than the few months ahead of the show working to get Cohen to the city: "'Why Milwaukee happened is because one guy, he flew the flag. (Jest) kept emailing the manager for three years and was really, really enthusiastic and passionate,' Elliott Lefko, vice president of talent for the tour's primary promoter, AEG Live Canada, told the *Journal Sentinel* in 2013. 'I thought, if he's so passionate . . . that's the kind of person we want to be in business with.'"

Peter arranged for the day of the show to be Leonard Cohen Day in Milwaukee. A proclamation was issued, in which the city joined "community members, Shank Hall, the Milwaukee Theatre and concertgoers in recognizing the many accomplishments of Leonard Cohen on Friday, March 15, 2013." The proclamation celebrated Cohen's career, including his inductions into the Rock and Roll Hall of Fame and the Songwriters Hall of Fame, alongside his Grammy Lifetime Achievement Award.

The show was one of the best—and most well attended—of all shows in Milwaukee that year. Between the opening song, "Dance Me to the End of Love," and "Closing Time" three hours later, more than 3,200 people basked in the sonic and visual wonderland created by Cohen and his band.

Peter, Karen, and Peter's mother watched the show from the fifth row. It wasn't entirely unheard of for Peter to watch a show from the front of the house, but it was a new experience to be approached by strangers before the start, during intermission, and after the show had ended.

People walked right up to Peter and thanked him for making the show happen. The gratitude continued rolling in for a couple of weeks after the show. A neighbor rang his doorbell to tell him how much they'd appreciated the show. Two people sent handwritten notes addressed to Peter at Shank Hall. One arrived after the show. The other, from a woman who described herself as "having reached an age even higher than Mr. Cohen's," arrived two days before. In it, she told Peter of a concert Cohen had played in Norway in the 1970s, where she was born and raised:

> I invited my then-teen-age niece to join me for the event. It became a most unusual evening. Police entered the stage, interrupting the performance, telling us that everyone had to leave because of some threat (a bomb). Nobody moved. Not until Mr. Cohen announced that he would continue the concert outdoors. And there, in the mellow light of that summer evening, the generous Mr. Cohen found a grassy knoll where he played his guitar and sang (without a microphone) for all of us who stayed. Over the many years since then, Leonard Cohen often gives concerts in Norway, where he is extremely popular. My niece always goes to these well-attended events. (I, on the other hand, having settled here in our area, have not had those opportunities.) So I now consider myself fortunate to attend next week's concert.

Her niece, she added, was flying in from Norway to attend the show with her.

On the Cohen forum, a fan wrote that the Milwaukee show "was magic. Every seat was filled. Everyone in the audience treated it as sacred, yet jubilant. I have never seen Leonard so connected and jovial at the same time."

Peter wanted more of that magic, and he had some ideas about where to look for it. He was in regular contact with Steve Martin—not the

Peter's framed copy of the poster advertising his Leonard Cohen show hangs on the wall of his home office.

Leonard Cohen on stage at the Milwaukee Theatre on March 15, 2013. PHOTO FROM THE ESTATE OF ART ELKON

comedian and actor, but an agent with whom Peter had been working since the mid-1980s. As he had done with Leonard Cohen's agent, Peter would check in regularly with Steve to find out if Pink Floyd guitarist David Gilmour had plans to tour again. During one of these check-ins in September of 2013, Steve mentioned that Gilmour was getting ready to record and tour. The North American tour would likely be just four or five cities, as his past tours had been. Milwaukee wasn't even a contender.

David Gilmour wasn't just one of Peter's favorite acts. He was a legend. Peter knew a Gilmour show in Milwaukee would be a huge coup. He hurried down to Central Library in downtown Milwaukee and spent an afternoon in the Humanities Room scrolling through old issues of local papers on microfilm. He found every article and ad connected to shows Gilmour had played with Pink Floyd in the 1970s and 1980s and then sent them to Steve. He sent twenty-five articles about the band's three local shows—June 22, 1975; June 15, 1977; and September 30, 1987—along with a letter to Steve, pleading for a Milwaukee date. He promised to give Gilmour and his wife, Polly, private tours of anything they wanted to see in Milwaukee, including "our world-class public museum, art museum, Calatrava and Zoo." Knowing that Gilmour owned a houseboat called the *Astoria* that they kept on the Thames River, Peter offered to rent a houseboat so David and Polly could go out on Lake Michigan. "David will say Milwaukee was the best night of the tour," Peter promised. Steve, via email, declared the package "a fantastic pitch," adding that he was going to London in a few weeks and would personally deliver it to Gilmour's manager. Peter waited. For two years.

In late March of 2015, during another routine check-in call, Steve mentioned to Peter that Gilmour would be releasing a new record that fall, *Rattle that Lock*, and touring in 2016. He noted that Chicago was proving to be a challenge because they couldn't get three nights that would work on account of the NHL's Blackhawks and the NBA's Bulls playing intermittent games that week. "What if we do Milwaukee as one of the Chicago dates?" Peter asked.

Steve asked Peter to check the availability of a March date at the Bradley Center. That would be during basketball season, but since the Bucks' schedule for 2016 hadn't been finalized, much less announced, the Bradley Center said they'd be able to make it work. Steve let Peter know the date had been confirmed by Gilmour's people and to stand by for on-sale and ticketing information. Peter couldn't believe his luck.

After several weeks passed without a word from Steve, Peter picked up the phone. "Ugh," Steve said. "I hate to tell you this, but David changed his mind. He had originally planned to do nine cities, but now he only wants to do four and as many dates in those cities as he can. He doesn't want to move, so it's going to be Toronto, New York, Chicago, and LA." Peter was in the process of letting out a deep, disappointed sigh when Steve spoke again. "But, you know, Chicago is still a problem because of the building scheduling."

Venues big enough to accommodate acts like David Gilmour are frequently the home bases of NBA or NHL teams. They have the right of first refusal on all dates, and it takes a lot of logistics to arrange a season's worth of games, most of which get figured out far in advance of the moment when schedules are released to the public. It's in those intervals between the schedules being finalized and being announced to the public that other events, like concerts and graduations, can be slotted in. Steve asked Peter to check with the Bradley Center about another date, this one in April. Again, he went to the center's scheduling department, and, again, Doug Johnson, the executive in charge, offered up a date for a possible David Gilmour show.

Inspired by Leslie West, Peter rolled up his sleeves and appealed directly to Gilmour. In the letter he wrote, he expressed how much Milwaukee would love to host a David Gilmour show. He referenced Pink Floyd's *Animals* tour show in 1977 and pointed out that lots of big acts—like the Rolling Stones and Elton John—set up a home base in Chicago, play their Chicago dates, and go from there to other venues around the region. He even offered to fly Gilmour to and from Milwaukee by helicopter, which, he added, would take less time than it would for him to play his song "Echoes." Peter vowed to donate all of the show's profits to the charity of Gilmour's choice if he didn't have a good experience, and, finally, he offered Gilmour his own most prized possession—his father's US Army Air Corps uniform from World War II.

That last offer was an indicator of how much Peter knew about the artist he was courting. Gilmour was an aviation enthusiast who, in addition to being a licensed pilot, had once owned a collection of vintage aircraft. Ultimately, Gilmour decided to stay in Chicago and play the Auditorium

While trying to convince Pink
Floyd guitarist David Gilmour, an
aviation enthusiast, to perform
in Milwaukee in 2015, Peter
offered him the Army Air Corps
uniform worn by his father,
Marvin Jest, in World War II.

Theater, a much smaller venue than the Bradley Center, but one he'd played
with Pink Floyd in the 1970s. Still, Peter heard that he had read the letter.
Which was something. He also got two free tickets to the Auditorium show,
where he sat across the aisle from Steve.

"The show was great," Peter said years later.

It was a little odd, because in the back of my mind, I was thinking
This should have been my show in Milwaukee. But these are legendary
people. They deserve to play where they want to play. And I could
keep on trying to change their minds, but at the end of the day, they
have a right to play where they want to play and, you know, I'm
still the biggest fan even though he didn't come here. But it's sort of
memorable. I was so, so close twice to getting the biggest show of my
life and career. So I hope that one day, he has another record in him
and he'll tour and maybe he'll think, you know, I've got to come and
do that Milwaukee gig for that guy.

≪ ≫

David Gilmour wasn't the only legend Peter had been trying to bring to Milwaukee around 2016. Since 2013, he'd also been courting Patti Smith, who'd last played Milwaukee in June of 1979. As with David Gilmour, her agent was a longtime associate—Frank Riley. He'd been the Violent Femmes' agent since 1982, so he and Peter knew each other well.

"Ah," Frank said, "Patti doesn't do many US dates. She does a lot of European dates."

Peter made an offer anyway, which was not accepted. The next time he asked, he offered more money. The time after that, he offered more yet. Finally, Frank responded that Smith and her band might do a short Midwest run. He asked Peter to check some dates in early 2017. When he found that March 9 was available at the Milwaukee Theatre, he made an offer, his best yet. Based on the conversations that resulted, it looked as if the run was going to happen and Milwaukee would be a stop.

Then came the Nobel Prize ceremony in Stockholm on December 10. Patti Smith, at Bob Dylan's request, was his stand-in. On his behalf, she accepted his Nobel Prize in Literature, delivering a speech he'd written and performing "A Hard Rain's Gonna Fall" at the Stockholm Concert Hall. As she was getting ready to sing the second verse of the song, which she'd been singing since she was a teenager, a song she knew "backwards and forwards," she suddenly froze. "Not 'forgot the words,'" she explained later to Norwegian TV host Fredrik Skavlan. "I froze. And when I think of it now, I still can do what I did—I covered my face. I was so humiliated and ashamed to fail."

Peter, who'd watched the performance, was convinced his this-close-to-happening Milwaukee date was doomed. "She's gonna get stage fright and never want to perform again," he told Karen. Yet, in that moment at the ceremony, Patti Smith simply owned what she was feeling. "I'm so nervous," she said and asked the musicians to start again from just before the moment where she'd been unable to continue. The rest of the performance was flawless. The next day at a postceremony event, still feeling raw and terrible, she told Skavlan, something powerful happened. "All the Nobel laureates, all the people were so happy and so happy to see me and so happy that I was so flawed and had had such a rough moment because, they told me, they all do, and they felt a kinship," she said. "And, you know, I learned a great lesson from that."

Meanwhile, Peter, who knew from his past dealings with Frank that confirmation of the show would come via email, tried to focus on things other than his inbox. On Monday, December 19, an early Christmas present showed up. "Peter," Frank wrote, "Happy and pleased to officially confirm your offer, and this date Thursday, March 9, 2017, at the Milwaukee Theatre in Milwaukee, WI."

The rest of the email discussed coordinating an appropriate date for the public announcement and ticket sales—taking into consideration the fact that the news could get lost amid the December holidays, but also thinking about having enough lead time to maximize the time span between the announcement and the show. "What else can I say?" he concluded. "These will be some of the most exciting shows of 2017. And what a way to start the year. Thanks for the offer, thanks for the date and best on this show."

Peter let Tom Crawford, Piet Levy, and Dave Luhrssen know right away. Everyone else found out on January 2, 2017. The show was so special and Peter had worked so hard for it that he did something he'd done just a couple of times before: he put his own name on the show advertising. Instead of ACG presents, it was Peter Jest presents. Peter also arranged for March 9 to be Patti Smith Day in Milwaukee.

In the run-up to the show, he received an email from the Milwaukee Press Club. Jim Nelson, the deputy business editor at the *Milwaukee Journal Sentinel* and a member of the Press Club's board, was inviting Patti to the Newsroom Pub, where the Press Club displays more than two thousand autographed plaques dating back to the late 1800s. The Press Club wanted to add her autograph to its collection, which includes the signatures of notable people in the arts, culture, entertainment, politics, and journalism. The club wanted to honor Smith in part for her 2010 memoir, *Just Kids*, the story of her relationship with the late photographer Robert Mapplethorpe, which had won that year's National Book Award for nonfiction. This wasn't meant to be an event where fans could meet Patti; it would be a private event where the club would honor her legacy. Peter forwarded the request to Andrew Burns, Patti's tour manager.

On the day of the show, Smith, along with her band members Lenny Kaye and Tony Shanahan, showed up at the Press Club. "When Patti Smith comes to Milwaukee, we have to treat you like royalty," Tom Barrett, the city's mayor, said as he prepared to read the proclamation declaring March 9 Patti Smith Day in the city.

"I don't know why," Smith said, laughing, "but I'm happy." Her face was a study in joy as Barrett read the proclamation. The members of the small crowd, including Peter, applauded when Barrett handed Smith the plaque, then quieted as she addressed the room.

"I have to say that today is a very special day for me for two reasons," she said. "March 9, 1976, I met my future husband, Fred Sonic Smith, and so March 9 is a very special day for me. Also, it was the passing day of Robert Mapplethorpe, so I have two very pivotal things in my life that happened on March 9. So, I always look at this as a day to honor them and to be creative and productive," she said.

Peter was staying in the background as usual, when someone pointed him out and introduced him to Patti. But the really special moment for Peter happened during the second half of the two-hour show Piet Levy described in his review as "a fierce, purposeful show that honored the past, felt visceral and relevant in the present and will be remembered in the future." Patti Smith acknowledged him from the stage. "I'd like to thank

On March 9, 2017, Patti Smith was honored for her literary work and received a mayoral proclamation declaring it Patti Smith Day in Milwaukee. Present at the Milwaukee Press Club were (from left to right) guitarist Lenny Kaye, Smith, Peter, and bassist and keyboardist Tony Shanahan. PHOTO BY EROL REYAL

The phrase "Peter Jest proudly presents" at the top of this promotional Patti Smith poster reveals how special the show was to him.

PETER JEST PROUDLY PRESENTS HER FIRST MILWAUKEE APPEARANCE IN 38 YEARS!

Patti Smith
and Her Band
perform Horses

MARCH 9
8 P.M.

THE
MILWAUKEE
THEATRE

Tickets on sale at The Milwaukee Theatre Box Office, *ticketmaster* or by phone at 1-800-745-3000.

WMSE   ARISTA   ACG
ALTERNATIVE CONCERT GROUP

Patti Smith on stage at the Milwaukee Theatre. PADDY FINERAN / PADDYWILLSHOOTYOU

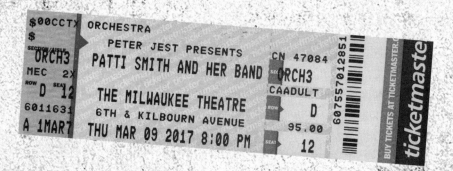

After the show, Smith's tour manager presented Peter with the set list, autographed by the band.

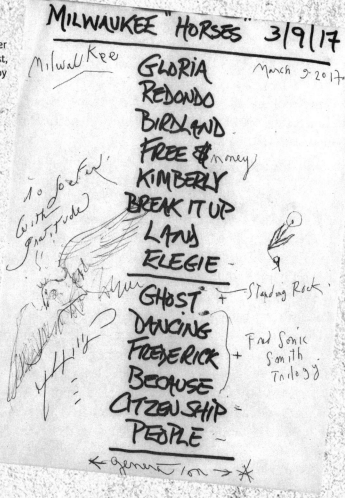

Peter, the promoter, for bringing me to this beautiful place," she said. "It sounds great, and he tried so hard and I really appreciate it."

Peter's mother wasn't there to hear it; Peter had brought her to see Leonard Cohen, but he knew that a Patti Smith show wasn't Kathryn's idea of a good time. His sister, Karen, and her husband, Jeff, were there, along with Peter's wife, Karen, to share that moment.

The March 9 set list included three songs Smith and her band rarely performed in sequence. These were played to honor Fred Smith, who died in 1994. The band performed "Dancing Barefoot," "Frederick," and "Because the Night." It ended with an encore cover of the Who's "My Generation." The first half of the show was a live, full-album performance of her 1975 release, *Horses*. Band members Lenny Kaye, on guitar, and Jay Dee Daugherty, on drums, had also played on the album.

At the end of the show, when Peter went to meet with Patti's tour manager, Andrew, to settle up, Andrew presented him with a signed copy of Patti's book and the show's set list signed by everyone in the band. He also shared that Patti wanted to make sure Peter hadn't lost money on the show. He hadn't.

The next morning, Peter got an email from Andrew. "Thanks for everything," it read in part. "Patti lost a silk type scarf multi color . . . same she wore to the press club I know she left press club with it. She might have dropped it in the Steve car? Or at hotel restaurant or the stratosphere lounge. At top of hotel . . . any chance to check. . . ." Andrew had already called the hotel, which he described as "less than helpful as I attempted to check if it was left there."

Peter knew Patti hadn't dropped the scarf in the "Steve car." Steven Gulke had been helping Peter as a runner for decades and would have notified him immediately. Peter called Andrew to let him know. That was when Andrew told him that the scarf had been a gift from Fred. Peter assured him that he would do everything possible to track it down.

He called the Wisconsin Center. They couldn't find it. He went there anyway and turned up nothing. He called Andrew to let him know. His next call was to the Hyatt, where Patti had stayed. They told Peter they'd checked their lost and found, and the scarf wasn't there. It wasn't that he didn't believe the hotel staff, but he had to see for himself. They were right. He called Andrew, who recalled that Patti had been at the café. "Maybe check there," he said.

"They're not open yet," Peter told him. "I'll come back when they are." Two hours later, Peter was at the counter, asking the woman behind it if she'd seen the scarf. She had, and suddenly it was in Peter's hand. He reached into his wallet to express his gratitude with a $20 bill.

"I found it!" he told Andrew. "I'm going to the UPS Store now and will overnight it to your show tomorrow in Pittsburgh."

To Peter, it was an example of the difference between an independent promoter and the behemoths that had gobbled up the live concert, ticket, and venue markets: "Some people might have said, 'I couldn't find it, now I'm off to the next thing.' But as an independent promoter, it's my responsibility to take care of my performer, to personally check things. They mean a lot to me, even after the money has been paid and the business is done. It was important to me to make sure that she got this very special item back."

Peter also got something unexpected, although not totally surprising. Andrew had told him to look for "something special in the mail." Two weeks later, a package arrived at his house. In it was a *Horses* tour jacket.

Less than one year after bringing Patti Smith to Milwaukee, Peter found himself chasing down another major act—one that had meant a lot to him as a kid. In November of 2018, Peter saw online that Mott the Hoople was playing a handful of US dates in 2019. Ian Hunter, the band's lead singer, had been a bright star in Peter's musical solar system since the 1979 solo release of *You're Never Alone with a Schizophrenic*. Peter had promoted several Ian Hunter solo dates at Shank Hall and, before that, UWM. If the band came to Milwaukee, it would be the city's first Mott the Hoople show in forty-five years. When they'd last been to Milwaukee in 1974, they were touring behind their album *The Hoople* and riding high, especially for a band that had been on the verge of breaking up two years prior. In 1972, after their first of three critically acclaimed albums failed to garner commercial success, David Bowie, a fan of the band, heard about their impending breakup. He wrote "All the Young Dudes" for them and produced the single, which went to number three on the British pop charts and became a hit in the US. He then went on to produce their album of the same name. The band's Milwaukee Auditorium show had turned out to be

Hunter's last tour with the band before he left to embark on a solo career; it had also been the band's first with guitarist Ariel Bender.

Getting one of the dates on the 2019 tour would be a big deal, so Peter called agent Frank Riley. "We need a lot of money," Frank responded. "Is there an audience in that market to justify the play? If it were to happen, it would be April 1. Let me know what you really think . . . and then we can get into it."

Peter wanted it to work. He checked his calendar and groaned. The Pabst Theater Group had booked Pink Floyd drummer Nick Mason and his band at the Riverside Theater the same night; the fan base for both acts was the same. Hunter had played Shank Hall in the early 2000s with drummer Steve Holley, who'd also been in Paul McCartney's band Wings. Both were on the Mott the Hoople tour, along with Bender and veteran keyboard player Morgan Fisher.

Peter had a relationship with Holley outside of his connection to Ian Hunter. The first time Holley had played Shank with Hunter, Peter had asked him to sign one of the prizes he'd won back in high school—a six-foot version of the cover of the Wings album *Back to the Egg*, which now held a place of pride on the wall of his office. Two of the other musicians on the album had also played Shank and signed it: Holley's fellow Wings member Lawrence Juber and John Paul Jones of Led Zeppelin, who hadn't been in the band but had played on that record. Holley had played Shank a few times since—once again with Hunter and also with Dar Williams.

Peter did the calculus in his head. Hunter was seventy-seven. This was a now-or-never proposition. He went for it, booking the band into the Milwaukee Theatre for April 1, the same venue they'd played in 1974 under a different name. In January, he began the process of organizing a mayoral proclamation to make April 1 Mott the Hoople Day. And, now that he knew about the Milwaukee Press Club's plaque collection, he reached out to James Nelson to see if they'd be interested in adding a set of Mott the Hoople signatures. They were, and, as they had done for Patti Smith, the Press Club hosted a reception at the pub where a mayoral proclamation declaring April 1, 2019, Mott the Hoople Day in Milwaukee was read and presented to the band members.

After the one-hundred-minute set, Hunter thanked the close to two-thousand-strong crowd who'd come out on a Monday night. "We love

Peter's April 1, 2019, Mott the Hoople show at the Milwaukee Theatre was the band's first stop on its US tour, and it turned out to be one of the last shows the band ever played. MILLER HIGH LIFE THEATRE

coming to Milwaukee," he said. "You're the only place in the country where, when you get here, people thank you for coming. Nobody else does that."

Peter sent an email to Frank the next day to express his gratitude. "You have sold me 2 shows that will be talked about for ages here: Patti Smith and Mott the Hoople," he wrote. "I really appreciate the faith you showed in me to present these 2 shows. I did get a nice email from Ian and Trudi (Mrs. Hunter) thanking me for the date and hospitality. Hopefully you received good feedback as well."

Frank's reply? "Really happy that both of these shows landed in Milwaukee. On some level, hard to believe. On the other . . . well deserved. An especially great way to begin the Mott run of shows, too. . . . Thanks for all of your efforts, thanks for the opportunities. . . . To many more. . . ."

Rolling the dice to bring Mott the Hoople to town the same night as Nick Mason had been risky, but it was the right decision and, it turned out, not just because everyone came away happy and the show had been profitable. The band played seven more dates on that tour, ending at the Beacon Theater in New York on April 10. They were scheduled to play another set of eleven US dates in the fall, but Ian Hunter was diagnosed with severe tinnitus, and they canceled the remaining shows.

In 2019, the *Journal Sentinel* ran a story by Piet Levy about twenty-seven artists or bands who hadn't played the city in more than a decade, if ever. He name-checked Peter as the promoter who'd been responsible for bringing "long-overdue Milwaukee returns" for Smith, Cohen, Mott the Hoople, and others.

Peter didn't spend a lot of time thinking about how far he'd traveled, career-wise. Three decades earlier, he'd literally fought City Hall to open his own venue. Now, he was part of Milwaukee's music establishment, with a solid track record behind him and dreams of even more big shows ahead. What he, and everyone else in his industry, couldn't know at that point was that they were all about to face the biggest challenge of their careers.

13

Shutdown

One of Peter's longest professional relationships was with the At-A-Glance company. He'd been using At-A-Glance spiral-bound datebooks since he started ACG back in 1982. Each month's 11-by-17-inch spread contained a strip down the left side of the page showing the previous month at the top, the current month (highlighted), and the five following months. The rest of each page was divided into boxes for every day of the month containing six ruled lines. Peter listed his Shank Hall shows on the top line and anything happening at other venues around the city on the bottom lines. A name highlighted in yellow denoted an ACG show.

The datebooks were windows into not just Milwaukee's concert scene but also the national music scene of a particular era. The acts, and the venues where they were playing, painted a picture of who was hot, who was starting out and hoping to become hot—or, at least, hoping to have a viable career—and who was still touring in the later stages of their career. Most of the entries were music related, but others—like football games, vet and doctor appointments, and sometimes just a name, like Mom or Karen—provided glimpses into the other aspects of Peter's life.

On the second day of January in 2020, Peter's datebook listed a 10:00 a.m. meeting with his accountant. He was never one to put off filing taxes, and his materials were always in order when he handed them over to Putterman & Watchmaker well before the April filing date. Peter had everything segregated—Shank Hall and Alternative Concert Group were separate entities with separate identities and separate tax returns. When the accountant gave Peter the forms he'd need to give Tracy, Keith, Dave, and the rest of his Shank crew, he'd hand over Karen's W-2 and the rest of the paperwork for his and Karen's joint return. There wasn't a lot—he and Karen lived pretty modestly. Their biggest expenses were pet food and vet bills, and Peter's biggest extravagances were his "Gold Package" Packer's season tickets and his annual fishing trip. Between 1934 and 1994, the Packers had played two to four games a year in Milwaukee, rather than their home base of Green Bay. The team sold season tickets for that cluster of games, which they called the Gold Package (tickets to Lambeau Field games were sold as the Green Package). Season-ticket holders have always been allowed to transfer them to family members. For people whose parents or grandparents acquired them back in the day, season tickets to Packers games are regarded as valuable family heirlooms. In 1994, after their last of three games at County Stadium in Milwaukee, Peter's father divided his season tickets among his children. Peter got a pair, for which he has continued to pay annually ever since.

The day after his tax appointment was Peter's first Shank show of the year, Albert Lee on January 3. His first ACG show was January 31, Leo Kottke in Oshkosh. Another Leo show was planned in April at Vogel Hall in Milwaukee. Neither one of them knew then that Leo's January show would turn out to be ACG's only one that year.

Recording engineer David Vartanian (second from left), Violent Femmes bassist Brian Ritchie (in sunglasses), and Peter attend a Packers game at Lambeau Field and are possibly the only fans not wearing anything green or gold.

Everything on Peter's calendar went according to plan in January and February. Acts came to Shank and the other venues, played their shows, then traveled to their next gigs or went home to sleep. Meanwhile, another story was slowly evolving, moving from a single line in American newspapers to front pages and television news A-blocks. In early January, the World Health Organization (WHO) issued a Disease Outbreak Report about what health authorities in Wuhan, China, had described as "viral pneumonia." The report included information about the number of cases, their clinical status, and what Wuhan was doing to address it, along with a risk assessment. That was quickly followed by a report announcing that the outbreak was the result of a novel coronavirus. On February 1, the WHO announced that the virus would be named COVID-19. By then, the US Centers for Disease Control and Prevention had begun screening passengers on flights coming from Wuhan to airports in New York and San Francisco, with plans to expand to other US airports, and they had identified seven cases of COVID-19 in the US. Among those were two Illinois residents with no recent travel history.

On Valentine's Day, Paul Cebar played at Shank Hall. The next day, an Associated Press story on page 10 of the *Milwaukee Journal Sentinel* reported that cases of the new virus were rising in China, noting that "hundreds of infections have been reported elsewhere."

On February 25, the same day the *Milwaukee Journal Sentinel* ran a locally written story with the headline "Spread of Coronavirus in US Could Close Schools," Piet Levy, the paper's music and pop culture reporter, published a brief piece announcing a September show featuring Nick Cave and the Bad Seeds. "It's the band's first appearance in the city since playing the same venue in 2014," he wrote. "That show, like this new one, presented by veteran local concert promoter and Shank Hall owner Peter Jest, was the band's first headlining appearance in Milwaukee."

Peter's Facebook feed had always been a place where he posted photos of pets needing homes, shows he was excited about promoting, and the usual random thoughts people share on social media. On March 11, he made a pitch for not panicking. "Please still go out and see live music and support small businesses," he posted. "Wash your hands and keep enjoying life. If we are confined to our homes we will be bored then hire monkeys as entertainment then they learn to talk from us and revolt and then we have the Planet of the Apes—so please go out so we can avoid becoming the Planet of the Apes—we all saw the movie and saw how it ends."

The next night, the Bel Airs played Shank Hall. Earlier in the day, Wisconsin's governor, Tony Evers, had declared a public health emergency. There were six cases of COVID-19 in the state; border states had increasing caseloads. Peter posted that he felt like he'd bought a round-trip ticket— outbound on the *Hindenburg* and returning on the *Titanic*. On March 13, the night Albert Cummings played the club, Evers ordered the closure of all Wisconsin public schools. Peter posted a list of six postponed and two canceled shows. By the next night, when Duke Tumatoe played Shank, people were already committing to staying home. That day, Peter posted a list that had grown to thirty-seven postponed and nine canceled shows. The audiences for Albert Cummings and Duke Tumatoe, about fifty each, were far smaller than they would have otherwise been. Both touring acts were grateful just to play.

"Thank you for keeping the date," Cummings told Peter on Friday before heading out. The next night, Duke Tumatoe told Peter he didn't need to pay the full amount they'd agreed on when he booked the date. "Hey," he told Peter, "I just appreciate you staying open."

Peter covered his panic with jokes on his Facebook feed, but when the only musicians at Shank were the ones looking out from the framed publicity photos covering the club's walls, he gave in to what he was feeling. On the sixteenth of March, he posted this:

This is a difficult time for the live music industry. To help venues please keep buying tickets if you are able for future shows. The cash flow will help. Most of Shank Hall's employees have other jobs. To the workers who do not, we will do maintenance around the club to get them hours. For musicians, buy their CDs and merch online. When everyone re-opens please go out more and spend more on live entertainment.

To the Government please help[!] Most of the small independent club, bar and restaurant owners have never received government help—now is the time. We need a moratorium on any taxes owed [and] bills that prohibit beer delivery if a distributor is owed over 15 days. . . . We need banks and especially loans backed by SBA to be held till business can open. Utilities need to help and let people pay what they can—we have no income, we cannot pay normal overhead.

Peter's usual routine included regular check-ins with friends in and out of the music industry—he and Leslie West talked at least once a day and often more than that. He chatted weekly with agents Jerry Lima in California and Brian Hill in Nashville. But when the pandemic shut down the industry, he began checking in on local musicians—like John Sieger, Pat McCurdy, and Paul Cebar—and other promoters, like Bob Babisch at Summerfest and Gary Witt at the Pabst. Everyone was talking about what they were seeing, what they were doing, and how they were handling things. Booking new shows wasn't on anyone's to-do list. Everyone was just trying to figure out how to reschedule the shows they'd already booked, with no clue of how to even begin speculating about time frames. It was hard for Peter to make sense of anything on his calendar, because each show had either "postponed" or "canceled" scrawled across it.

And Peter had no income to pay the bills that kept coming. Among those were expenses associated with 1434 North Farwell Avenue. As his second five-year lease was sunsetting in 1999, Peter had bought the building from Jim Wiechmann. Because of the way his two loans on the building were structured, the Small Business Administration would cover the mortgage payment on one loan while the club was closed due to the pandemic, but Peter was still responsible for the other loan and utilities. He also owed several media outlets for ad buys he'd committed to for shows that were no longer happening and liquor distributors for alcohol he'd ordered. No shows. No income. No answers. He had no idea how or when he'd be able to reopen, and neither did anyone else.

Karen's job at Children's Hospital continued uninterrupted, with one major change—her office was now an upstairs bedroom at home. Her employment situation was the difference between them slowly falling behind and falling into complete financial ruin. While they both enjoyed their work, they were a two-income household out of necessity. On top of that, Peter had employees whose livelihoods were entirely dependent on the continued viability of his business.

In early March, two dozen people in Nashville were killed when a tornado roared through the city. Peter fired off an email to Fiona Prine to see if she, John, and the boys were okay.

"We are," she responded. "Thanks for checking on us. Love you both."

On March 29, Peter emailed again to check in on the family. In an instant reply from Fiona, Peter learned that John was in the hospital and very ill with COVID-19. She wanted Peter to know before the news became public. "Pray for him," Fiona wrote. "He loves you. I love you."

The last time Peter had seen the Prines was in May of 2019 when John had performed two Wisconsin shows, one in Madison and one in Appleton. Fiona had brought a fancy bottle of wine so they could celebrate Karen's successful surgery. After reading Fiona's email about John's illness, Peter's first instinct was to pick up the phone. But he knew Fiona had to be overwhelmed by what was happening, so he responded by email, then told Karen. Only then did he make a call to Mitchell Drosin. They talked regularly, with Mitchell keeping Peter apprised of John's condition until April 7, the day he died.

"We were both crying," Peter recalled. "[John] was like Mitchell's best friend. I mean, John would not do dates if Mitchell had something going on. You never hear that—a tour manager telling the act, 'Hey, I'm going on vacation this weekend' and John saying, 'Well, we won't work that weekend.' That's how close they were."

The next day, Peter reposted Arlo Guthrie's tribute to John Prine, in which Guthrie described the last gig he and John had played together, a 2005 show at the Botanic Gardens in Denver. Peter had flown to Colorado to see the show. In his final paragraph, Arlo captured the essence of the man Peter loved so much: "He was warm, considerate, and willing to put up with the never-ending demands of being a nice guy. I got the feeling that he would've been the same guy no matter what he was doing—and he didn't need to be onstage. He just found himself there and did the best he could with it."

As devastating as it was to lose John, the impossibility of a funeral gathering made his death even harder to bear. Rituals, especially those around major milestones, mattered to Peter. He'd flown to Florida for John's surprise sixtieth birthday party, he'd hosted his parents' fiftieth anniversary party at Shank Hall, and he'd thrown parties for all of Shank's milestone anniversaries. In supporting friends facing life's more difficult moments, Peter's behavior and actions mirrored those of his parents. Marvin Jest's tender consideration for friends and family dealing with illness and tragedy hadn't been about setting an example. It was simply a part of his makeup,

Owning a club means always having a place to host private parties. The fiftieth anniversary of Peter's parents, Marvin and Kathryn, in 2005 was a big one. In 2021, the family gathered again when Peter hosted his mother's ninetieth birthday party.

a trait his youngest son had absorbed. Prior to the pandemic, Peter would drive his mother to hospitals and rehab centers to visit friends of hers who were ill or recovering. And in 2017, Peter had made a trip to visit his longtime friend Leon Redbone, who had been diagnosed with dementia and stopped performing a few years earlier. It was, although Peter didn't know it then, the last time he'd see Leon before his death in 2019.

When the father of his friend Kevn Kinney died, Peter, who was fresh out of the hospital after a bout of blood poisoning, showed up at the funeral wearing black attire and an IV pack. Now, he could only memorialize John Prine at home, wearing clothes with his friend's name and picture on them. Peter and Karen grieved together. It was months before he could bring himself to listen to a Prine record.

≪ ≫

Frank Marino had been scheduled to play Shank Hall the night Governor Evers's stay-at-home order was set to expire, April 24. With COVID-19 still raging in the state and elsewhere, Evers extended the order to May 24. Then the state Supreme Court blocked the extension, letting it expire and functionally opening the state in late April 2020 while keeping schools shut. COVID-19 cases and deaths were continuing to rise, a metaphorical finger in the eye of the court. Venue owners knew that emerging personal and political fights about whether masks prevented viral spread or whether COVID-19 had come from a market or a laboratory weren't going to result in a rush to see live performers in crowded spaces.

While Peter watched the state fight over COVID-19 restrictions, Dayna Frank, owner of the Minneapolis music venue First Avenue; Rev. Moose of Marauder, a creative marketing firm with strong ties to the independent venue community; and Gary Witt, an executive at Pabst Theater Group, launched NIVA—the National Independent Venue Association. NIVA's main aim was to ensure that independent promoters and venues survived the pandemic; its first priority was to make sure they were included in any federal and state aid packages aimed at COVID-19 relief. By June, sixty-seven Wisconsin venues had joined the two-thousand-strong group, ACG and Shank Hall among them. That same month, two US senators—Republican John Cornyn of Texas and Democrat Amy Klobuchar of Minnesota—introduced the Save Our Stages Act. The bill's passage would provide $16 billion in relief money for independent movie theaters, museums, and live-music venues affected by the pandemic.

On October 14, 2020, instead of welcoming the California Honey Drops to Shank Hall, Peter was poring over an announcement by the Wisconsin Department of Administration (DOA). The agency was awarding up to $15 million in grants to any live-entertainment venue, defined as "a business which generates 33% or more of its revenue through direct ticket sales or direct event charges for the production or presentation of live music, other entertainment or large conventions or meetings."

The submission deadline was October 29, just over two weeks away. Grantees would be notified in November. To be eligible to apply, a business needed to prove financial need, show that live entertainment (or hosting large conventions and meetings) was a central component of its business, and define the area and customers served. No entity would receive more than $500,000 or 25 percent of their 2019 ticket sales (whichever was less). To be eligible in Wisconsin, a live-entertainment venue also had to be a sole proprietorship or other entity doing business in Wisconsin, current on taxes, in good standing, and owned by a Wisconsin resident (if owned by a single owner). Applicants had to write a statement explaining the pandemic's impact on the venue's operations and services and tie that explanation to financial need, the degree to which producing or presenting live music was a component of its goals, and the value of the venue's presence in Wisconsin, including who it served.

Peter completed and submitted the proposal. In early December, he posted an update on his Facebook feed that included a reference to the funding. About Shank Hall, he wrote,

> We have a few shows scheduled yet in March and April, but realistically may not be opening in May. It simply is not safe to open up for live entertainment. My staff and the professional bands we book are 100 percent behind us as we do not want to kill anybody for a show. The staff is hanging in there. A few have other jobs, a few have been putting in a few hours cleaning the club and others are on unemployment—but all are safe. We did receive some money from the state to help with some of the overhead, but this year is still bad with the tremendous amount of overhead we have.

It's what he and other venue owners and promoters had been doing since the pandemic shutdown began—working with artists and managers to keep pushing out existing dates. The industry standard seemed to be four months out from the previous postponed date.

In early December, Shank Hall was awarded $57,178.14. Alternative Concert Group, Peter's main source of income, got nothing. The reason ACG had been passed over, as far as Peter could tell, was that it did not own a permanent venue. The DOA's website claimed that "the program was only available to owners and operators of venues which produce or present live music, other entertainment or large conventions or meetings." Because ACG produced events across the state at various venues, it did not qualify for aid. Worse, Live Nation, the Beverly Hills–based behemoth, had been awarded upwards of $395,000 from the state of Wisconsin. Peter had been sure, given that the state's benchmark to qualify for the grant was 33 percent in ticket sales and that ACG's revenue was 100 percent ticket-based, relief was on the horizon. He'd felt especially confident given that the pandemic had driven ACG's gross income from an expected $955,000 from twenty-five shows in 2020 to an actual $16,000 for one.

He vented his frustrations on Facebook:

> The state of Wisconsin will be wiring $395,000 to Live Nation in their Beverly Hills office. Live Nation Worldwide, who also owns Ticketmaster, is the same company that single handedly killed independent promoters, gave us the $50 service charge and $20 beer. We are wiring them $395,000! At least Live Nation CEO Michael Rapino can maybe reupholster a couple of his private jets with that money. Meanwhile we got zero. We are stealing our neighbors Sunday paper to look for a 2 for 1 Arby's coupon and driv[ing around in a] 2010 Yaris that needs reupholstering. If the State of Wisconsin gives them this money, I have no confidence in NIVA getting money from the federal government as I now think Live Nation will get all that money too. The rich get richer and Republican or Democrat, no one seems to care about the small businessperson.

But Peter did more than howl at the moon online. In addition to pressing his lawyer, David Halbrooks, into service to help him file an appeal and point out the disconnect, he contacted his legislators, the Wisconsin NIVA group, and anyone else he could think of who might listen. When the final list of grantees was released by the DOA on December 30, ACG was awarded $196,782.

That same month, the Shuttered Venue Operators Grant was included in the $2.3 trillion COVID-19 relief bill passed by Congress and signed into law by President Donald Trump. That grant provided $16 billion in federal aid for live-entertainment providers, including venues, promoters, and museums. Anyone operating on or before January 1, 2019, was eligible to receive an individual grant for 45 percent of their gross earned revenue or $10 million (whichever was less) for the year.

The grant was administered by the Small Business Administration. No one knew what kind of documentation would be required, so business owners got busy gathering everything. Which turned out to be a good idea, because the only thing the SBA didn't seem to want was the broom of the Wicked Witch of the West and the shrubbery from *Monty Python and the Holy Grail*. Peter and his Shank staff spent a lot of time at the shuttered club during the first part of 2021 going through the contents of the twenty-four-pack beer boxes where he stored his annual records and receipts. The SBA changed the information about exactly what was required to apply three times between when it released the initial application requirements on March 5 and the August 5 deadline.

Along with 2019 and 2020 tax returns—and a document authorizing the SBA to obtain copies of those returns directly from the IRS—the list of what to submit included floor plans, employee and payroll information, proof of a sound and lighting system, local government information on pandemic restrictions, lists of venues where shows were promoted, contracts and show listings, marketing materials and box office information for all shows in January or February of 2020, and, for those who had more than ten events planned in 2019, a listing of the ten the applicant thought best represented their organization.

Shank's paperwork was more straightforward than ACG's for one very simple reason: Shank didn't have to refile its taxes. Alternative Concert Group did. Independent promoters like Peter, who booked artists into spaces they didn't own, generally walked away from a show with a check in the amount of ticket sales minus that venue's associated costs. Take, as an example, an ACG show at the Barrymore Theater in Madison. Peter would book the artist and rent the space. The Barrymore would take care of the rest, including printing posters and tickets and arranging for sound, lights, and cleaning—everything involved with the show minus the advertising. At the end of the night, Peter would get a check that reflected what was left after those expenses were deducted, the net revenue from the show. His accountant used that number when documenting Peter's income for tax purposes, a long-established common practice. But now he and every promoter in his position had to refile their taxes using gross revenue, then show and subtract their expenses. The final amount owed or refunded didn't change. It was simply a matter of showing, in a different and more complex way, how it had been reached. The problem was that there was a sixteen-week interval between filing and processing those amended returns because of the pandemic's impact on day-to-day operations at the IRS, an already-stressed federal agency.

By the time Peter submitted his applications in early April of 2021, both he and Karen had gotten their first vaccines. Peter was still pushing shows to future dates, but it seemed as though it would soon be possible to stop scrawling "Postponed" or "Canceled" over the entries in his calendar. He had no sense of when any money from the Shuttered Venue Operators Grant would arrive, but the Wisconsin funds had been a huge relief. He was able to catch up on the mortgage and utility payments for Shank and pay down the credit card debt that had helped carry him, Karen, and his businesses through. More important, he was able to repay the people who'd helped him through 2020.

Peter had a long history of borrowing and repaying money, dating back to his teenage use of his father's credit card to buy the concert tickets he resold to his Milwaukee Lutheran classmates. He always paid his father back before the bill came due. As an adult, his method of dealing with any kind of short-term cash flow situation was to issue an IOU in the form of a postdated check. If he needed more time, he would ask his payee to hang on to it. His payment history on those short-term loans was as good as it had been when Marvin was his main creditor. Paying back the friends who'd helped him and Karen through a difficult time felt hopeful, like better things were on the horizon. Not new beginnings, but some kind of return to what had been lost. He'd also made improvements to the club—a tangible message to himself, his staff, and the public that they would reopen. Along with installing new bathrooms, Peter bought a new digital marquee to replace the old one. He gave Shank's stash of giant letters to Leslie West for the Rave, whose freestanding marquee used the same style letters. He also bought new lighting and purchased the sound system he'd been renting for as long as the club had been open.

On June 23, 2021, Peter and Karen's ninth wedding anniversary, the Shuttered Venue Operators Grant money landed in Shank's and ACG's bank accounts. The club was set to open that week, and ACG had its first show—King Crimson at the Miller High Life Theater—scheduled for August 31. The uncertainty of the past fifteen months had not completely disappeared. Peter knew things might never return to a version of life before the pandemic, but the money he received—a direct result of three decades of relentless work and meticulous recordkeeping in a business that often rewarded that kind of effort with penury—meant that he, Karen, and his Shank crew would be able to ride it out. The fact that he suddenly had more money than he'd ever had at one time was something. But, Peter noted, it wasn't everything.

"I mean," he said, "I'd still trade all of it to get John Prine back."

14

In It for the Long Haul

On June 25, 2021, Shank Hall opened for its first show in fifteen months. Peter limited capacity to a smaller number than what the city required. He ended up with a crowd of one hundred to hear Milwaukee natives Goran Kralj and Daniel Rey of the local alt-rock band the Gufs. Rey opened the show with an acoustic set. The crowd sat, silent, listening to the first live music played on the stage beneath the miniature Stonehenge sculpture in more than a year. The final notes gave way to an extended moment of quiet between the end of the song and the beginning of the applause. It was almost as if the people in the crowd were collectively groping for the answers to a pop quiz on what to do at a show. By the end of the night, as Kralj and Rey were winding up their set, people seemed to have remembered how to be an audience. They let loose approving whoops and shouts of "yeah!" midsong. Peter's pandemic Facebook rant about how concertgoers should keep their phones in their pockets had clearly been forgotten by anyone in attendance who may have seen it. A smattering of raised phones were aimed at the band, and a small crowd that included one intoxicated person being held up by a cadre of friends was dancing directly in front of the stage.

Two months later, on August 31, Alternative Concert Group was back. *Slow* was Peter's adjective of choice to describe ticket sales for his first ACG gig, a King Crimson show at the Miller High Life Theater, with the Zappa Band as the opening act. Tickets weren't enough to get a person in, though—anyone without a vaccine card and ID would be turned away. It was not an unreasonable requirement, since voluntary gatherings of more than small crowds still felt like a gambler's game; with the Delta variant surging, COVID-19 case counts were on the rise again. Masks, however, were optional at the theater. Most showgoers opted out, but a healthy number of attendees were masked up. All in all, it felt like a respectable turnout for a Tuesday night at an indoor venue in the earliest stages of a post-shutdown world. The crowd ranged in age from twentysomethings to retirees, and at least one attendee could be heard talking about ivermectin. It was one of the few indoor shows on King Crimson's twenty-eight-city US tour.

Less than a month later, Peter acted on a promise he'd made to himself during the pandemic: if there was something he wanted to do or see and had the chance, he wasn't going to wait. He'd been too young to see Van Morrison in Milwaukee in 1973, and there was no certainty he'd get the chance to see him at a hometown venue. Peter flew from Milwaukee to San Francisco, where Jerry Lima picked him up from the airport. From there, they made the ninety-minute drive to Napa. Van was playing a

King Crimson has a strict "no photography" rule during shows, but once a show is over, the band stays on stage after the lights go up, and everyone—including the band—takes photos. At this August 2021 show at the Miller High Life Theater, valid vaccine cards were required for entry; masks were optional.
PHOTO BY AMY T. WALDMAN

show that night at Oxbow River Stage, a four-thousand-seat outdoor venue; his daughter, Shana Morrison, and her band were opening. Peter and Shana had been friends since 2018. Because of COVID-19 protocols, Peter knew he wouldn't be able to meet up with her, but he texted after the show to let her know how much he'd enjoyed her set and finally getting to see her dad play live. Jerry dropped him back at an airport hotel after the show, the halfway point between Napa and where he lived in Monterey, and at 6:00 the next morning, Peter was on a flight home. The whole trip had taken just twenty-four hours. Though he hadn't been able to see Shana, he had met up with Ron Kaplan, Jerry's former colleague and Van's agent.

The Violent Femmes and Peter were both in Milwaukee for an October 22 hometown show at Miller High Life. Flogging Molly opened. Afterward, Peter and Karen met up with Brian Ritchie and his wife, Varuni Kulasekera, at the Pfister Hotel. The next day, the Femmes were playing the Armory in Minneapolis, the last show of their tour. Peter and Karen flew up the day after that show to meet Brian and Varuni and see the Rolling Stones at US Bank Stadium. That show was also mask-optional, but Brian and Varuni stayed masked—they would be going home to Tasmania soon. Australia's strict COVID-19 restrictions had kept the country's caseloads among the lowest in the world, and travelers returning to the country were subject to quarantine if they posed even the slightest risk of having brought the virus with them. After the show, Peter and Karen hitched a ride back to Milwaukee on the Femmes' tour bus.

On November 1, an intimate crowd gathered at Shank Hall to hear Brian Ritchie and the Zen Gardeners (Femmes drummer John Sparrow and percussionist Mike Kasprzak). The instrumental set, featuring Brian on wooden flutes, included a cover of "Ue e Muite Aruko," which he introduced as probably "the only song that became a number one hit in the US and was a protest song against the US occupation of Okinawa." Released in Japan in 1961, the song was retitled "Sukiyaki" for its US/ UK release, topping pop charts in multiple countries under a name one journalist compared to retitling "Moon River" as "Beef Stew." The Zen Gardeners also performed an acoustic version of "Oysters Stomp," a Ritchie-composed tune originally recorded by The Break, a four-piece band including Ritchie and members of the bands Midnight Oil and

Several tours'
worth of
Violent Femmes
backstage
passes.

Hunters & Collectors. At the end of the night, after thanking the audience, Brian singled out his host before closing the show with Ornette Coleman's "Lonely Woman": "Thanks, Peter Jest, for supporting live music in Milwaukee for years, even before there was no pandemic, for more than twenty years—how long, Peter?"

"Thirty-two years," Peter responded.

Two weeks later, Peter was at the Pablo Center in Eau Claire with Leo Kottke and drummer Dave King. It was the second of a two-show run—the first had been at Milwaukee's Vogel Hall. The Vogel Hall show had been postponed four times during the pandemic; the Pablo Center show was supposed to have happened in April, but it had been moved back when cases spiked. The good news was that, like many of the shows Peter had booked back in 2019, it was finally happening. A grateful audience (that included guitar maker Kevin Muiderman, who'd built the guitar Leo was playing) listened in rapt silence to the music, laughing appreciatively at the stories Kottke told in between.

Shank was open, and ACG was back on its way to some semblance of up-and-running. But the losses and changes the pandemic had wrought were also front of mind. John Prine was dead. Arlo Guthrie had retired.

Peter had struggled financially, but the state and federal money his businesses had received had put him in an unexpected position. He wasn't independently wealthy, but for the first time in his career, he had some latitude to take bigger risks—not a thing he'd had the luxury of even imagining in the three-plus decades he'd been promoting shows. That latitude, he realized looking back, was really the result of one person's faith in his ability: Steve Mandelman. Steve could have used Peter when he needed him, then made himself scarce when his own career as a promoter had ended in disaster. Instead, he'd continued to support Peter's efforts to bring live music to UWM, and he had made himself available to do what he could to help as Peter launched a career of his own. At least twice a year, they got together for lunch. Steve, who was now living with Parkinson's disease, was thinking about getting back into the promotion game. He wanted to do a five-city run of shows to benefit Parkinson's research. Peter didn't exactly try to talk him out of it, but he knew that Steve's time away from promoting shows had insulated him from being fully aware of how much the music business had changed since 1982.

At various points during Shank Hall's life, Peter had been approached by different people to host benefits and had always made the club available to them. The Violent Femmes held one in 1991 to help people displaced by the Norman apartment building fire and another in 1994 for WMSE, a local college radio station. Steve's idea spoke to Peter on multiple levels. Here was a chance to honor the person who'd opened the door that made his career possible, and the pandemic money meant that even if the benefit shows didn't turn a profit, he'd be able to absorb the loss. He and Karen also committed to a personal donation of ten thousand dollars. Steve and his wife, Harriet McKinney, chose the charity; Peter chose the cities and performers.

≪   ≫

Over the years, Peter had worked with the offspring of many musicians who were household names. These included Ginger Baker's son, Kofi Baker; John Bonham's son, Jason Bonham; Harry Chapin's daughter, Jen Chapin; Bob Dylan's son Jakob Dylan; David Gilmour's son Matt Gilmour; Arlo Guthrie's children Sarah Lee, Abe, and Cathy Guthrie; Paul and Linda McCartney's son, James McCartney; Van Morrison's daughter Shana

Morrison; Willie Nelson's children Lukas and Amy Nelson; Sting's son, Eliot Sumner; James Taylor and Carly Simon's son Ben Taylor; Loudon Wainwright III and Kate McGarrigle's daughter, Martha Wainwright; and Hank Williams's grandson Hank Williams III. A few he knew very well, like the Guthrie kids. Others left lasting impressions that had nothing to do with music. The first time James McCartney played the club, in June of 2016, he surprised Peter with a question he'd never been asked before. The temperature was in the high 70s, and Peter was in short sleeves. Before they headed into the club, he gave James a heads-up about his giant poster board of the *Back to the Egg* album cover. "I don't want to scare you or anything," Peter told him, "but there's a big picture of your parents in my office."

"Oh, that's nice," James said. They walked toward the back of the dimly lit room, James stopping at various points along the way to study the photos on the wall. Peter matched his pace, not wanting to rush him. Then, James asked a question: "Are you on heroin?"

If he hadn't already been standing still, Peter would have stopped where he was to process what he'd just heard. Brow furrowed, he followed James's eyes, which were aimed slightly downward at Peter's right arm. Peter placed a finger by an uneven row of raised red bumps. "This?" he said. "It's eczema."

"Oh," James said. "I'm just asking. I'm not trying to judge or anything."

Peter had nothing to say. He didn't really know how to tell James that if there were Grammy awards for "Club Owner Least Likely to Do Drugs" Peter would be a multiyear winner. Instead, he said nothing. When James played Shank again the following April, there was no mention of heroin.

It was 2018 when Peter booked Shana Morrison and her writing and performing partner Kim McLean for the first time. They opened for a pair of Leo Kottke shows, one at the Barrymore in Madison on June 8 and the other at Vogel Hall in Milwaukee the next night. Ripping a page from his John Lee Hooker days, Peter had borrowed his mother's car to meet them at the airport. Shana lived in Northern California and Kim in Nashville; neither had played Wisconsin before. Peter was their ride between the airport, the venues, the hotels, and the cities. All that time in the car together could have been silent or awkward. Instead, the trio discovered enough common ground to forge lasting friendships. "One of the things I

Kim McLean
(left), Peter, and
Shana Morrison
(right) after one
of their 2018
shows with
Leo Kottke.

like about promoting the kids of famous rock stars is that at my age, I'm
sort of right in between," Peter reflected later. "I'm more the age of the
kids than their famous rock star parents, so it's sort of fun to hang around
with them. Shana is a hoot."

Peter had also shared something with Shana in 2018 that was both
personal and professional. For a lot of touring musicians, the only parts
of a city they ever see is the bed where they sleep and the venue where
they're playing. From this perspective, one city looks pretty much like
another, and after a while, they all blur together. Peter kept that in mind
when he had the chance to fetch an artist from the airport, and he always
took the scenic route, from 794, over the Daniel Hoan Bridge to Lincoln
Memorial Parkway, with its expansive view of Lake Michigan. Showing
off his hometown made him happy. Milwaukee is a beautiful city; he
loved all it had to offer and was proud to share that with an act when he
could. Both Shana and Kim liked what they were seeing and experiencing
as Peter drove them around the city. When he finally shared with Shana
that he'd long wanted to see her father play Milwaukee, her response
was something along the lines of "Milwaukee's great. My dad would
love it here."

"I've been trying for over ten years and getting nowhere," Peter admitted. When Shana said she'd talk to her dad, Peter expressed his gratitude, and they moved on. The Leo Kottke dates were successful, onstage and off. Leo had played some dates with Van in the 1970s and shared with Shana his memories of those days. After, everyone returned to their respective corners of the world. Peter and Shana kept in touch, emailing back and forth every few months. As promised, she talked to her father about Milwaukee, reporting back that he was interested. Whether that would translate into an actual date was another question.

Doing a Van Morrison show after more than a decade's worth of regularly rejected offers would be a peak moment in Peter's career. So, he did what he'd done with David Gilmour, trekking down to the central branch of the Milwaukee Public Library again to visit the Humanities Room and spend an afternoon going through microfilm, pulling all the ads and articles connected to Van's 1973 appearance. Then, he made an appointment to see the old *Bugle American* collection. The *Bugle American* had been one of Milwaukee's small alternative papers at the time, and it had covered the show. The issues were not on microfilm but, rather, housed in the library's Rare Books Room. When Peter read the article, he discovered that a very tiny Shana had been in Milwaukee with her father that night. When she toddled into the room where the *Bugle American* interview was happening, the reporter remarked that she was cute and asked what her name was. Van told him it was none of his business and ended the interview. Peter gathered up a bunch of materials—including a scan of the *Bugle American* interview and several articles extoling the virtues of Milwaukee—and sent them to Jerry at the agency that represented Van and, because of the story about her, to Shana.

Peter didn't have to sell Shana on Milwaukee, and he knew that she and Kim would be a good fit for his Parkinson's shows. He liked them as people and as performers—it would be fun to see them again. Additionally, they would work well with Jen Chapin, an artist he really wanted to bring back to town. Steve Mandelman had been the reason she'd played Shank in 2007. As a promoter, Steve had worked a lot with, and been close to, Jen's late father, Harry, making her a natural choice for Steve's benefit. Also, Jen's cover of Van Morrison's "Into the Mystic" had garnered upwards of 450,000 views on YouTube—another reason Shana would be a good fit for the double bill.

Peter chose three cities and three dates in early March. Shana and Jen would play Shank Hall on Thursday, then the Grand in Oshkosh on Friday, and then the Barrymore in Madison on Saturday. In a press release announcing the shows, he noted that both artists had "blazed their own trails in the music business." Shana Morrison's "roots-inflected vocal style," the release read, was "more straight-ahead pop/rock than her father's," while Jen Chapin's "jazz-inflected story songs explore community and shared meaning." Chapin would be performing with her husband, Grammy-nominated acoustic bassist Stephan Crump, and guitarist Jamie Fox; Kim McLean was returning to play with Shana.

Steve and his wife, Harriet, were among the small but robust crowd of about fifty that showed for the first performance at Shank Hall, a pretty respectable turnout for a Thursday. Shana and Kim opened the show and were followed by Jen and her band. Both artists played a few of their fathers' songs, in addition to their own. Then, all five musicians shared the stage for a performance of Stevie Wonder's "Higher Ground." After the show, Peter transported Shana and Kim to their hotel in his mother's car. Jen and her crew had their own minivan. The next day, they'd meet in Oshkosh. The two weekend shows drew larger crowds—about two hundred in each city.

The Parkinson's benefit was one of the first Shank Hall events that hadn't been a rescheduled pandemic show. Another big one had taken place about a week earlier. Peter had made a conscious decision to marry Karen at a venue that wasn't his own, but one of the upsides of owning your own club was never having to figure out where to host your mother's birthday party. On February 20, Shank's digital marquee featured a picture of Kathryn Jest and the message "Happy 90th." The club had been transformed into an event space; the crowd was four generations of Jests. There were flowers, pink and purple balloons, and cloth-covered banquet tables festooned with confetti. A giant banner hung behind the merch counter, which had been converted into a gift table and cake station. Peter's siblings and their offspring helped themselves to pulled pork, lasagna, bread sticks, stuffed shells, meatballs, artichoke dip, and tiny caprese salad skewers from the buffet table along the wall. He'd cued up an afternoon's worth of cartoon videos for his great-nieces and great-nephews, but he needn't have bothered—the kids spent the afternoon dancing and playing on Shank's empty stage.

≪ ≫

It's a dicey thing to be the child of an icon going into your parent's business, and Peter had seen enough to be aware of the hazards, as well as the signs that someone, regardless of their connections, was doing it right. In September of 2022, Tommy Prine, John's youngest son, played his first solo show at Shank Hall. The date coincided with the release of the first single, "Ships in the Harbor," off his upcoming album. Before the show, Peter and Karen took Tommy and Charlie Overby, Tommy's opener, to dinner at Maharajah. Over Indian food, they caught up on how things were going with Fiona, Tommy's siblings, and his life as a newlywed and touring musician. John Prine and Al Bunetta had founded Oboy Records in 1981 after John's contract with a major label ended and he decided to start his own. Tommy, Peter observed, had made a conscious decision to begin his career without leveraging any family connections. "He's done everything on his own," Peter said. "He got his own record deal and his own management."

Tommy's set revealed him to be a singer who wasn't trading off his father's name but also was not running away from it, performing a collection of meditative and beautifully written original songs in a rich baritone. The last verse of "Ships in the Harbor" begins with, "When I'm by peaceful waters" a paraphrase of the opening line from his father's song "Lake Marie." It ends with "I'd do anything just to talk with my father."

Tommy was among a younger generation of acts hitting the stage at Shank Hall. Like their older counterparts, they appreciated the stage and its history—and the joke behind the name. "We're going to turn up the amps to eleven on this one," ukulele virtuoso Jake Shimabukuro told a crowd of about seventy who'd come out to hear him on a Monday night in September. "I'm gonna be Nigel, who're you going to be?" he asked Jackson Waldhoff, his bass player, then launched into a spoof version of Spinal Tap's "Stonehenge."

"I had to! It's right there!" he said, laughing and pointing to the eighteen-inch sculpture above his head as the audience cheered. Peter wasn't at the club that night, so he missed Shimabukuro thanking Marvin Jest for his military service, and Peter for the club and the show. "We can't wait to come back to Milwaukee!"

Acts come and acts go, but the eighteen-inch replica of the Stonehenge stones is always center stage at Shank Hall. PHOTO BY AMY T. WALDMAN

On a night in 2022, the club was full of revelers celebrating the fortieth anniversary of the *Crazy Shepherd*, an upstart alternative paper that would later become the monthly *Shepherd Express*. Two local bands, the Swivels and Bristlehead, shared the bill. Former *Shepherd* staffers passed out souvenir T-shirts, and a dark-haired woman urged everyone to partake of the giant birthday cake she'd brought to celebrate her husband's sixtieth birthday. As the party wound down, she approached the bar where Peter was sitting with a friend.

"I'm Stephanie, and I just wanted to say thank you so much for letting me bring the cake. Your staff was so helpful when I called to set everything up," she said. "We've been coming here since you opened—we love Shank Hall and we come here all the time, and I just have to tell you how impressed

I am with everything you've done. You probably don't remember me, but I was there when you were first starting out at UWM. I was a student there, too—part of the activities board at the union and a member of the concert committee."

Peter blinked, stared, kicked his friend under the barstool, and accepted the compliment. They watched Stephanie and her husband exit the club, at which point Peter explained what had just happened. She had been the concert chair who'd sat silently by while the Union Activities Board chair told eighteen-year-old Peter that national acts wouldn't want to play UWM. "You should probably thank her the next time she comes in," his friend said. "If she'd stood up for you, we might not be here."

When Peter Jest walked into the Union Activities Board office that day in 1982, he was fresh off an important lesson about the risks associated with promoting shows and confident in his ability to navigate them. The students he met there were among the first in what turned out to be a long list of people who did not take him seriously—an easy mistake if you judged him by his appearance. Peter always had been a guy you'd pass on the street without looking twice. His walk could best be described as a purposeful waddle, and his go-to wardrobe was a rumpled concert T-shirt (usually with John Prine's name on it) and jeans. At a 2022 Porcupine Tree show he'd promoted—the only show of the band's ten-city US tour not promoted by Live Nation—Peter sported a T-shirt that looked as if it had lost a fight with a wood chipper. He did not become one of Wisconsin's longest-lasting independent promoters or the owner of one of Milwaukee's oldest music clubs based on his fashion sense. It wasn't because of his charm, either. Peter was never "Midwest nice."

He did, however, have a strong moral compass and no tolerance for anyone who challenged it. He was fearlessly, unapologetically himself. There was no artifice or pretense—and that was a rare thing in a business heavily populated by Rolex-wearing schmoozers who lived for access to fame and talent. It was the reason that some of his devoted friends were, in fact, famous musicians. Those people have a serious nose for suckups, and they recognize talent when they see it. Peter was as good at his job as they were at theirs, and the performers he became friends with recognized and appreciated that. Like them, Peter had to fight hard to earn his place in the music ecosystem.

As Peter's friend Leslie West observed, Peter "started with nothing, and everything he's gotten, and done, he's done completely on his own, doing it his way or the highway and it's worked for him. Nobody landed a big pile of money in his lap and said, 'Here, go out and be this great concert promoter.'" That determination—and hardheadedness—earned him the respect of his peers, many of whom remember the teenager who wanted to be a concert promoter.

Bob Babisch, who retired as the entertainment vice president of Summerfest after forty-five years, remembered his first encounter with Peter:

> He was this brash kid that decided he wanted to be a concert promoter. I was already at Summerfest, and I thought it was fascinating how he really wanted to be in the concert business, and you know, in that business, there's not a lot of glamour. People think it's glamorous, but it's really not. It's putting shows on. It's not the easiest thing in the world to do. And you can make some money and can lose a ton. You can make money for five shows and lose it all on number six—it's devastating sometimes. But people that fall in love with it really fall in love with it. And Peter fell in love with it. He believes in the bands he books, and if he likes the music, he wants to promote you. It's not just a quick buck for him.

Peter was still in high school when he first crossed paths with Randy McElrath, who would, more than a decade later, become his boss at Cellar Door. As Randy explained,

> I had started—as most of the promoters had—a concert club for high-volume ticket buyers. You could join a club for a fee, and you were guaranteed to get better-than-average tickets. That was always hazy—how good they were depended on the acts. But one of the first people, you know, that signed up, was this guy. I hadn't really looked at the name at first, but he printed everything in very big letters. And it was hard to miss any time he had a letter. And in addition to ordering tickets, he complained a lot. That's probably how I came to know him. He complained that, you know, he wasn't getting the best seats all the time.

Decades later, Randy openly admired that teenage kid who figured out how to make a life in a business notorious for chewing people up and spitting them out. He described Peter as "gracious, but overworked. Being a club owner, doing all that, that much entertainment, you have to have calluses some places, because you get all sorts of stories. You're not always running into the most professional people that you have to deal with. And to be doing what he's done as long as he has? My God, what endurance!"

According to Peter's attorney and friend, David Halbrooks, "The genius of Peter is he works so hard to put together experiences that nobody else appreciates. Peter provides experiences in that room that you can't have anywhere else." Genius? Maybe. Tenacious? For sure. Driven by a passion for live music? Without a doubt.

When does Peter plan to retire from promoting? Never. He hopes to be doing a handful of shows even into his seventies. He's a realist—he knows that some of his longtime acts and friends won't be around to promote for too much longer. Gordon Lightfoot died on May 1, 2023, and George Winston died on June 4 of that year. Still, Peter remains hopeful about

Gordon Lightfoot
and Peter after one
of the last shows
they did together.
PHOTO BY KAREN JEST

pie-in-the-sky shows, like David Gilmour and Van Morrison. And he won't stop looking for the next emerging artist—someone with that rare combination of talent and loyalty—who might choose to work with him.

The music industry continues to change, and in some fundamental ways, Peter Jest remains the same—an independent promoter and club owner in a world where independent promoters and club owners are increasingly scarce. But he's susceptible to change, too. Way back in the beginning, his entire life had revolved around shows. Shows will always matter to him, but now Peter's life is also filled with friends, family, pets—and fishing. Who knows what changes, and what music, the next decades may hold.

BOBBY TANZILO/ONMILWAUKEE

Acknowledgments

A lot of people think writing a book is a high-wire solo act, and honestly, a large part is exactly that. But it's also collaborative, in sometimes surprising ways. You reach out to a stranger by email, and they give you a piece of information that saves you from committing a giant faux pas in an upcoming interview. An old friend asks about your book, then hooks you up with a bunch of people to interview. Your bestie shares the book-tracking spreadsheet she created. I could go on, but you get the idea.

So, with that said, I'll start by saying thanks to Ethan Silverman and Jeff Klepper for looking at a very early incarnation of the first three chapters. I owe Ethan big-time for the advice that led me to the Wisconsin Historical Society Press. Excellence is too small a word to encompass the experience of doing a book with them. It's more of an "I died and went to book-publishing heaven" kind of scenario. As for Jeff, I knew I was on the right track with the tone of this book when he said, "I like it, but maybe you should get him addicted to drugs. It needs more drama." I said, "It's nonfiction. Peter's real." Which leads me to Shauna Singh Baldwin, who cautioned that I needed to make sure there was conflict and a through-line. I owe both Shauna and Jeff for stressing the importance of giving Peter's story a plot and a narrative arc.

Thanks to my writing master class peeps—Aleta Chossek, MacKenzie Harris, Beth Huwiler, Judy Nelson McKee, Sharon Nesbit-Davis, Kim Parsons, Sara Rattan, Anne Rooney, Jeaneé Sacken, and our fearless leader, Judy Bridges—for helping to make sure that people outside of Peter's world would have a clear picture of life inside it; and to my brother-in-law

Tommy Hahn, who has played at Shank and who gave me an insider's view of that experience that helped inform this book, prompting me to ask Peter about things I wouldn't have thought to ask and things he wouldn't have thought to tell me. Also, a shout-out to Jim Owczarski, Milwaukee city clerk, for help with Common Council meeting dates and agendas.

To Christina Ward, for a crash course in book titles and covers; to Veronica Rusnak, for reality checks and moral support; to Michele Wucker, for that spreadsheet and all-around best-friend stuff; to Debby Waldman, writing inspiration, cheerleader, and best sister ever; and to Morgan Schidler, whose coaching, encouragement, and Hustle & Play calendar/planner/book-for-creating-the-life-you-want helped me figure out how to balance a publishing deadline and a full-time job.

To the interviewees named in the bibliography and to those of you who took the time or were willing to be interviewed and didn't end up there: Paul Cebar, Kevn Kinney, and John Sparrow; to Danny Zelisko, for the Alan Parsons show and the opportunity to see another promoter at work; to Barbara Elkon, who made her late brother Art's amazing photo archive available because I couldn't forget the photo he posted on his Facebook feed after the Leonard Cohen show; to Erik Lawrence, who, in addition to being my friend since before we were old enough to drive, closed the loop with Arlo Guthrie and connected me with Tom Roberts and Paul Cebar; and to Holly Gleason, whose book *Prine on Prine* wasn't finished when I reached out to her, but who helped make that chapter better nonetheless.

To my Good Hope Library crew (Alexis, Amelia, Dana, Ian, Jannis, Jasmin, Jessica, John, Joycelyn, Kevin, Kyle, Mark, and Nia) for support, cheerleading, and patience while I worked on this book, and to the members of Tribe Waldman/Frolkis/Wishart/Huber/Tyler/Haack/Smith/Twohig/Atwell/Sinden for their constant support.

To Kate Thompson, who plucked my book proposal off of her slush pile, trusted me when I said it should be written in the third person, and never pressured me to work faster; to Liz Wyckoff and Kaitlyn Hein, a writer's editorial dream team; to John Ferguson, production editor extraordinaire; and to everyone else at the Wisconsin Historical Society Press who had a hand in creating this book.

To Dave Luhrssen, for being the Peter and Amy Whisperer.

To Gene: True North, Best Friend, Emotional Support Human.

To Marvin and Kathryn Jest, whose support was not conditioned on understanding.

And finally—and with love—to Peter, who trusted me to tell his story.

—Amy T. Waldman

This book would not have been possible if not for the people who believed in my ability to do what I wanted to do as a career—especially when I was just a hundred-pound, teenage kid with braces who most people thought had no business being in charge. In particular, thanks to Steve Mandelman, who took me in at just seventeen years old to help on shows, and to Bob Babisch, who hired me at nineteen.

Thanks to Kristine Foate, who, as a sales rep at WQFM, gave that eighteen-year-old kid credit to run ads. To the agents Fred Bohlander, Steve Martin, Frank Riley, and Elizabeth Rush, who trusted me with their clients even at my young age. To Brian Ritchie, for coming up with this book's title and being such a great friend on and off the road.

To the late John Prine—so honored I was your Wisconsin promoter but more honored we were friends. To Arlo Guthrie—so many shows and fun times together with you and your kids, and I'm likewise honored we are friends. To the late Leon Redbone—you were one of a kind, and I am still laughing when I think of you. To Leo Kottke—thanks for turning around and making that show in 1985. We've done more than sixty shows since then and still counting. Sorry about the bird noise. To Fiona Prine, for approving of Karen and being there for us in that difficult time. To Beryl Handler, thank you for allowing us to visit with you and Leon—that was very special.

To Christopher Guest, Michael McKean, Rob Reiner, and Harry Shearer for giving Shank Hall its name. To my dedicated staff, especially Tracy Roe who has been there from almost day one. You are a special person to me, and I would not want to own Shank Hall without you in charge. To David Edwards, for always being there and taking care of the bands and the club. Thanks for helping me share memories, Mitchell Drosin, Brian Hill, Jerry Lima, and Leslie West.

To my sister, Karen, and brother-in-law, Jeff Worgull, who thought I was the family dog on their first date.

To Dave Luhrssen, who's been with me from the beginning.

Special thanks to Amy Waldman, who had patience with me and was able to pull some good stories out of me. Thank you for making this book happen.

And especially to Karen Eckert Jest, for making my house a home and filling it with even more pets than I could imagine and for being my partner through so many of these stories.

—Peter Jest

John Prine signed a copy of his last album, *The Tree of Forgiveness*, to Peter's mom: "Thanks for the yellow cake, Kay! Lots of love, John Prine."

Bibliography

At its foundation, this book is based on countless conversations, some recorded and many unrecorded, that occurred between me and Peter Jest. I spent the first year of my work on this project talking solely to Peter and going through materials he provided. When he wasn't sure about a date or when I needed more information about a particular event, I turned to print sources in library databases. Those sources are listed by chapter below.

Once I began expanding the narrative beyond Peter's recollections, I received a wealth of information from conversations and interviews with the following individuals: Bob Babisch, Peter Balistrieri, Victor DeLorenzo, Stephanie Drake, Mitchell Drosin, Arlo Guthrie, Tommy Hahn, Karen Jest, Robb Heilmann, Brian Hill, Kathryn Jest, Greg Koltermann, Leo Kottke, Goran Kralj, Jerry Lima, Jim Linneman, Steve Mandelman, Randy McElrath, Patrick Nedobeck, Mark Nerenhausen, Billy Prine, Fiona Prine, Brian Ritchie, Tom Roberts, Tracy Roe, Elizabeth Rush, Veronica Rusnak, Mike Stefaniak, Steve Sperling, William Stace, Leslie West, and Robert Weidenbaum.

I supplemented my knowledge of Peter's work with details from the International Entertainment Buyers Association website, https://ieba .org, and two pages from the Berklee College of Music website: "Career Communities: Concert Promoter," Berklee College of Music, www .berklee.edu/careers/roles/concert-promoter and "Career Communities: Talent Buyer," Berklee College of Music, www.berklee.edu/careers/ roles/talent-buyer. In order to cross-check and confirm concert dates and set lists, I repeatedly referenced "Past Shows," Barrymore Theatre, https://barrymorelive.com/past-shows/, Ron Faiola's website Milwaukee

Rock Posters, https://milwaukeerockposters.com, and various pages at Setlist.fm, "The Setlist Wiki," www.setlist.fm.

I also want to note that although Wikipedia has a controversial reputation as a source, it was a helpful starting place for my research on many topics in this book—particularly because most information there is linked to sources. The reference and discography sections of musicians' entries were especially useful during my initial stages of seeking out information on artists, songs, and albums.

Finally, I fleshed out most chapters with data from newspaper and magazine articles, websites, and various other sources, which are listed by chapter on the following pages.

Chapter 1: The Contest Winner
White, E. B. *The Trumpet of the Swan*. New York: HarperCollins, 2000.

Chapter 2: That Won't Work Here
Higgins, Jim. "Crowd Pleased by Spyro Gyra." *Milwaukee Sentinel*. March 8, 1983.

Infusino, Divina. "The Van Halen Show Starts with the Fans." *Milwaukee Journal*. August 18, 1982.

Joslyn, Jay. "Concert Canceled; Crowd Sent Home." *Milwaukee Sentinel*. October 20, 1982.

Strini, Tom. "Anka Cancels Concert at PAC." *Milwaukee Journal*. October 20, 1982.

Tanzilo, Bobby. "Milwaukee Talks: 1812 Overture Founder & Concert Promoter Alan Dulberger." OnMilwaukee. March 18, 2021. https://onmilwaukee.com/articles/mke-talks-alan-dulberger.

Chapter 3: Pissing Next to Batman
Maples, Tina. "Quite a Caper: Batman Wields His Peculiar Magic over a UWM Audience." *Milwaukee Journal*. November 26, 1984.

Strini, Tom. "Femmes' Music Cuts Barrier." *Milwaukee Journal*. May 3, 1984.

Chapter 4: On the Road
"About the Oriental Theatre." Milwaukee Film. https://mkefilm.org/oriental-theatre/about#history.

Chapter 5: Brushes with Stardom

Alternative Concert Group advertisement. *UWM Post*. October 31, 1985.

Christensen, Thor. "Concert at UWM Shows Pop Still Has Raw Power." *Milwaukee Journal*. September 26, 1988.

Foran, Chris. "Earth-Shaking Fire Guts East Side's Century Hall—in 1988." *Milwaukee Journal Sentinel*. April 19, 2016.

Chapter 6: Welcome to the Club

Clem. "Clementine's Calendar." *Milwaukee Journal*. November 3, 1989.

Drew, Mike. "New York Voices Rise to Occasion." *Milwaukee Journal*. November 29, 1989.

Higgins, Jim. "Live at Shank Hall." *Milwaukee Sentinel*. August 18, 1989.

———. "Shank Hall Materializes from Film Fantasy." *Milwaukee Sentinel*. November 3, 1989.

Maples, Tina. "Massive Tour Matches Stadium-Sized Ego, Talent." *Milwaukee Journal*. September 14, 1992.

———. "Shank Hall Debuts." *Milwaukee Journal*. November 3, 1989.

Shelton, Sonya. *Start Your Own Bar and Club*. 2nd ed. Irvine, CA: Entrepreneur Media Inc., 2006.

Tanzilo, Bobby. "Urban Spelunking: Shank Hall." OnMilwaukee. March 9, 2017. https://onmilwaukee.com/articles/urban-spelunking-shank-hall.

Chapter 7: The Music and the Mileage

Braun, Stephen. "Bill Graham, Concert Promoter, Dies in Crash." *Los Angeles Times*. October 27, 1991.

Christensen, Thor. "Peppers Turn Blender Up a Couple of Notches." *Milwaukee Journal*. October 23, 1991.

Kuipers, Dean. "Physical Graffiti." *Spin*. February 1990.

Snyder, Molly. "The Norman Fire Burns in the Memories of Former Residents." OnMilwaukee. December 29, 2021. https://onmilwaukee.com/articles/thenormanfire.

Chapter 8: Rising from the Ashes

Causey, James E. and Dave Tianen. "Shank Hall Damaged in Blaze, Owner Considers Closing Down." *Milwaukee Sentinel*. September 14, 1992.

Crawford, Tom. "WMSE Programming Philosophy." WMSE. www.wmse.org/wmse-programming-philosophy/.

Christensen, Thor. "Shank Fire Leaves Hole in Nightclub Scene." *Milwaukee Journal*. September 18, 1992.

———. "Shank May Rise from the Ashes." *Milwaukee Journal*. October 2, 1992.

Harrington, Kevin and Mary Carole McCauley. "Fire Damages Shank Hall." *Milwaukee Journal*. September 13, 1992.

Luhrssen, Dave. "The King of Clubs." *Wisconsin: The Milwaukee Journal Magazine*. September 5, 1993.

Maples, Tina. "Massive Tour Matches Stadium-Sized Ego, Talent." *Milwaukee Journal*. September 14, 1992.

———. "Like a Mighty Phoenix, Shank Soars Back into the Nightclub Scene." *Milwaukee Journal*. December 11, 1992.

———. "A Brighter, Larger, More Beautiful Shank Rises from the Ashes." *Milwaukee Journal*. December 18, 1992.

Chapter 9: Fine Milwaukee Water

Currin, Grayson Haver. "When Making Music Breaks Your Body." Georgia Public Broadcasting News. December 4, 2021. www.gpb.org/news/2021/12/04/when-making-music-breaks-your-body.

"Enabling and Running a Soundboard." WikiHow. Updated June 20, 2023. www.wikihow.com/Set-Up-a-Sound-Board.

Iwasaki, Scott. "The E Chord Changed Leo Kottke's Life Trajectory." ParkRecord.com. June 9, 2019. www.parkrecord.com/entertainment/the-e-chord-changed-leo-kottkes-life-trajectory/.

"Leo Kottke Bio." Red Light Management. www.redlightmanagement.com/artists/leo-kottke/.

Mittelstadt, Austin. "What Does a Sound Board Do?" Channel Audio. October 1, 2018. Updated March 28, 2022. www.channelaudiogroup.com/single-post/What-Does-a-Sound-Board-Do.

Pugh, Megan. "Vessel of Antiquity: Influence, Invention and the Legacy of Leon Redbone." *Oxford American: A Magazine of the South*. March 19, 2019.

"Leon Redbone." *Contemporary Musicians*. Vol. 19. Detroit, MI: Gale, 1997. *Gale in Context: Biography*. Updated September 12, 1997. https://link.gale.com/apps/doc/K1608000932/BIC?u=milw97470&sid=bookmark-BIC&xid=0aafaaf2.

Chapter 11: Only Love

Bonyata, Phil. "Rain Can't Damper the Irish Spirit." Concert Live Wire.
www.concertlivewire.com/fleadh.htm.

"Chicago Bulls at Milwaukee Bucks Box Score, January 16, 1998." Basketball-
Reference.com. www.basketball-reference.com/boxscores/199801160
MIL.html.

"Guinness Fleadh, Jun 12, 1999." Concert Archives. www.concertarchives.org/
concerts/guinness-fleadh.

Hoekstra, Dave. "Remembering John Prine." DaveHoekstra.com. April 7,
2020. www.davehoekstra.com/2020/04/07/remembering-john-prine/.

"How to Make John Prine's Favorite Drink—'The Handsome Johnny'
Cocktail." Distillery Trail. April 15, 2020. www.distillerytrail.com/blog/
how-to-make-john-prines-favorite-drink-the-handsome-johnny-cocktail/.

"John Prine Setlist at Riverside Theater, Milwaukee, WI, USA, Jun 10, 1999."
Setlist.fm. Updated June 8, 2022. setlist.fm/setlist/john-prine/1999/
riverside-theater-milwaukee-wi-4384374f.html.

"John Prine's Concert History." Concert Archives. www.concertarchives.org/
bands/john-prine.

Rubach, Carly. "John Prine Telling Stories at the Marcus." *Urban
Milwaukee*. March 10, 2012. https://urbanmilwaukee.com/2012/03/10/
john-prine-telling-stories-at-the-marcus/.

Thank, Juli. "John Prine Announces New Album, Ryman Dates."
The Tennessean. February 8, 2018. www.tennessean.com/story/
entertainment/music/2018/02/08/john-prine-new-album-ryman
-auditorium-nashville-dates/316949002/.

Valdez, Christina Killion. "John Prine, an American Treasure, to Perform
in Rochester." Rochester, MN, *Post Bulletin*. June 20, 2012.
www.postbulletin.com/lifestyle/arts-entertainment/john-prine-an-
americana-treasure-to-perform-in-rochester.

Waddell, Ray. "Al Bunetta, Longtime Manager of John Prine, Dies at 72."
Billboard. March 23, 2015. www.billboard.com/music/music-news/
al-bunetta-longtime-manager-of-john-prine-dies-at-72-6509492/.

Chapter 12: Hope Springs Eternal

Aswad, Jem. "Coachella Promoter Goldenvoice Sues Live Nation for Trademark
Infringement Over Competing 'Coachella Day One 22' Festival." *Variety*.

December 14, 2021. https://variety.com/2021/music/news/coachella
-goldenvoice-live-nation-trademark-infringement-1235133099/.

Daley, Dan. "Clash of the Titans: AEG Presents vs. Live Nation." *Front of House Magazine*. June 6, 2018. https://fohonline.com/articles/the-biz/
clash-of-the-titans-aeg-presents-vs-live-nation/.

Gillis, Charlie, Brian D. Johnson, and Katherine Macklem. "Leonard Cohen Goes Broke." *The Canadian Encyclopedia*. Last updated July 7, 2014.
www.thecanadianencyclopedia.ca/en/article/leonard-cohen-goes-broke.

Greene, Andy. "Sharon Robinson Reflects on Touring with Leonard Cohen." *Rolling Stone*. July 12, 2017. www.rollingstone.com/music/music-features/
sharon-robinson-reflects-on-touring-with-leonard-cohen-194281/.

Levy, Piet. "Leonard Cohen Brings Meticulous Approach to Milwaukee Theatre." *Milwaukee Journal Sentinel*. March 13, 2013.

———. "Leonard Cohen's Final Milwaukee Show 'Remarkable.'" *Milwaukee Journal Sentinel*. November 11, 2016.

———. "Mott the Hoople Rocks First U. S. Show in 45 Years at Milwaukee's Miller High Life Theatre." *Milwaukee Journal Sentinel*. April 2, 2019.

"Leonard Cohen, Mar 15, 2013, Miller High Life Theatre, Milwaukee, Wisconsin, United States." Concert Archives. www.concertarchives.org/
concerts/leonard-cohen-e47521a3-6d2c-40ab-a374-7bea93672397.

Martin, Erin Lyndal. "Leonard Cohen: 14 March 2013—Milwaukee." PopMatters. March 28, 2013. www.popmatters.com/169771-leonard
-cohen-2495768458.html.

Mayor Cavalier Johnson (@MayorOfMKE). "The punk poet laureate returns." Twitter, March 10, 2017. https://twitter.com/MayorOfMKE/
status/840291107414147073?s=20.

"MOTT THE HOOPLE 74 US TOUR: Road Movie #1, Milwaukee 2019/4/1." Morganfjp. April 5, 2019. YouTube video, youtube.com/watch?
v=rvKEJZNDMD80.

Mueller, Kevin. "Patti Smith Returns to Milwaukee." *Milwaukee Magazine*. March 7, 2017. www.milwaukeemag.com/patti-smith-returns
-milwaukee/.

Patch, Nick. "Toronto Promoter Elliot Lefko Hits It Big in L.A." *The Canadian Press*. February 9, 2012. https://toronto.ctvnews.ca/toronto-promoter
-elliott-lefko-hits-it-big-in-la-1.766134.

"Patti Smith on Nobel Prize Performance: I Was Humiliated and Ashamed,
    SVT/NRK/Skavlan." Skavlan. October 17, 2017. YouTube video,
    www.youtube.com/watch?v=lVQ4UUWgs2Y.
Rytlewski, Evan. "Patti Smith Will Play Milwaukee for the First Time Since
    1979." Shepherd Express. January 3, 2017. https://shepherdexpress.com/
    music/on-music/patti-smith-will-play-milwaukee-first-time-since-1979/.
Sweetannie33. "Concert Report: Milwaukee, WI, March 15, 2013." Leonard
    cohenfiles.com. Updated March 17, 2013. www.leonardcohenforum.com
    /viewtopic.php? p=326748&sid=58a36edaaacdd570145f6ba4d5e096
    9d#p326748.

Chapter 13: Shutdown

Evers, Tony. "Gov. Evers Announces More Than $140 Million for Wisconsin's
    Tourism and Entertainment Industries." Office of the Governor, State of
    Wisconsin. June 24, 2021.
———. "Gov. Evers Awards More Than $27 Million in Grants to Event Venues
    and Live Event Small Businesses." Office of the Governor, State of
    Wisconsin. December 21, 2021.
Glauber, Bill and Ricardo Torres. "Wisconsinites Brace for Altered Daily Life
    Amid Coronavirus Pandemic, Fears." Milwaukee Journal Sentinel (online).
    March 15, 2020. jsonline.com/story/news/2020/03/14/wisconsin
    -coronavirus-people-brace-altered-life-amid-pandemic/5050538002/.
Johnson, Mark. "Spread of Coronavirus in U. S. Could Close Schools."
    Milwaukee Journal Sentinel (online). February 25, 2020. jsonline.com/
    story/news/2020/02/25/coronavirus-scenes-china-almost-certain-
    play-out-u-s/4870019002/.
Levy, Piet. "The Coronavirus Crisis Decimated Milwaukee's Spring Concert
    Season. Venue Owners are Worried for the Future." Milwaukee Journal
    Sentinel. March 18, 2020.
———. "Live Music Hit Hard by Gathering Restrictions." Milwaukee Journal
    Sentinel. March 20, 2020.
———. "The Coronavirus Pandemic is Devastating for Milwaukee Musicians.
    Here Are 11 Ways You Can Help." Milwaukee Journal Sentinel. March 20,
    2020.
———. "Concert Update Venues, Shows Affected by Coronavirus Pandemic."
    Milwaukee Journal Sentinel. March 27, 2020.

———. "10 Ways to Help Milwaukee Musicians During Coronavirus Epidemic." *Milwaukee Journal Sentinel*. March 29, 2020.

———. "'Everyone Is Jacked Up': After 14 Awful Months, Milwaukee Venues Get Ready to Host Concerts Again with Big Crowds, and without Masks." *Milwaukee Journal Sentinel*. May 27, 2021.

———. "FM 102.1 Hosting Auction, 24-Hour Radiothon with Rock-Star Guests to Help Struggling Milwaukee Venues." *Milwaukee Journal Sentinel*. July 7, 2020.

———. "Legendary Singer-Songwriter John Prine, Who Died of COVID-19 Complications, Had Strong Ties to Wisconsin." *Milwaukee Journal Sentinel*. April 7, 2020.

———. "Mike Hoffman, Milwaukee Music Scene 'Legend' from Semi-Twang and Yipes!, Dies at 67." *Milwaukee Journal Sentinel*. October 28, 2021.

———. "Shank Hall in Milwaukee Was Going to Reopen this Month. Now It Won't Happen Until February, at the Earliest." *Milwaukee Journal Sentinel*. August 11, 2020.

———. "'We're Talking About Life or Death': Milwaukee Music Venues Look to Allies, and Washington, to Survive the Pandemic." *Milwaukee Journal Sentinel*. April 30, 2020.

Luthern, Ashley. "Coronavirus Cancellations Rising—In State and Around US, Expect More Closures." *Milwaukee Journal Sentinel*. March 13, 2020.

Marley, Patrick. "Gov. Tony Evers to Order Wisconsinites to Stay at Home, Will Close Non-Essential Businesses." *Milwaukee Journal Sentinel* (online). March 23, 2020. jsonline.com/story/news/politics/2020/03/23/wisconsin-gov-tony-evers-issues-safer-place-order/2897821001/.

Moritsugu, Ken. "Virus Cases Rise, But Counting Method Questioned." *Milwaukee Journal Sentinel*. Februrary 15, 2020.

Moss, Marissa R. "John Prine Was in on the Joke All Along." *Billboard*. April 7, 2020.

Rytlewski, Evan. "Gov. Evers Announces $15 Million in Grants for 96 Wisconsin Music and Entertainment Venues." Radio Milwaukee. December 3, 2020. https://radiomilwaukee.org/story/milwaukee-news/gov-evers-announces-15-million-in-grants-for-wisconsin-music-and-entertainment-venues/.

"Shuttered Venue Operators Grants: Frequently Asked Questions." US Small Business Administration. January 27, 2021.

"Shuttered Venue Operators Grant: Application Checklist." US Small Business Administration. July 28, 2021.

Snyder, Molly. "New Sign for Shank Hall". OnMilwaukee. January 4, 2022. https://onmilwaukee.com/articles/shank-hall-new-signs.

Speer, Debbie. "Q's With: NIVA Founding Members Dayna Frank, Rev. Moose and Gary Witt." Pollstar. April 24, 2020. https://news.pollstar.com/2020/04/24/qs-with-niva-founding-members-dayna-frank-rev-moose-and-gary-witt/.

"Timeline: WHO's COVID-19 Response." World Health Organization. Updated March 20, 2022. www.who.int/emergencies/diseases/novel-coronavirus-2019/interactive-timeline#.

Yasharoff, Hannah. "#SaveOurStages: How the New COVID-19 Relief Package Will Help Entertainment Venues." *Milwaukee Journal Sentinel*. December 21, 2020.

Chapter 14: In It for the Long Haul

Bream, Jon. "Guitar Great Leo Kottke and Drum Master Dave King Form a New Minneapolis Super Duo." *Minneapolis Star Tribune*. November 26, 2021.

Cieslak, Kelly. "Music Groupie Turned Concert Promoter Honors His Mentor." *Wisconsin Parkinson Magazine*. April 21, 2022. https://issuu.com/kathleenhess/docs/wpa_magazine_spring_2022f3.

Levy, Piet. "Taylor Swift and 24 Other Acts That Haven't Played Milwaukee in More Than a Decade—Or Ever." *Milwaukee Journal Sentinel*. March 7, 2019.

Schultz, Blaine. "Jen Chapin, Shana Morrison to Play Parkinson's Benefit Shows in Wisconsin." *Shepherd Express*. February 15, 2022. https://shepherdexpress.com/music/music-feature/jen-chapin-shana-morrison-to-play-parkinsons-benefit-shows-/.

"Some Time with Shana Morrison." Green Arrow Radio. May 25, 2018. https://greenarrowradio.com//?s=shana+morrison.

Index

Note: Page numbers in *italics* indicate illustrations.

About the Authors

Amy T. Waldman is an award-winning writer and editor whose feature articles, reviews, profiles, and essays have appeared in the *Milwaukee Journal Sentinel*, the *Shepherd Express*, *Milwaukee Magazine*, *The Wisconsin Jewish Chronicle*, *Publishers Weekly*, *People*, the *Forward*, and *Reader's Digest*. She was also a reporter and lifestyle editor for the *Marshfield News Herald* where she wrote Fresh Sounds, a biweekly record review column. She is a reference librarian at the Milwaukee Public Library.

Peter Jest has promoted music in Wisconsin and the Midwest for more than forty years and is the owner of the Milwaukee music venue Shank Hall. This is his first book.

David Luhrssen is the author of many books on film and music, including *The Vietnam War on Film* and *The Encyclopedia of Classic Rock*, and coauthor of *Milwaukee Rock and Roll, 1950–2000* and *Brick Through the Window: An Oral History of Punk Rock and New Wave in Milwaukee*. He is managing editor and film critic of Milwaukee's weekly newspaper, the *Shepherd Express*.